Silent PAIN

FINDING GOD'S COMFORT FOR
YOUR HIDDEN HEARTACHES

KATHY OLSEN

D1508903

NAVPRESS ◢
A MINISTRY OF THE NAVIGATORS
P.O.BOX 35001, COLORADO SPRINGS, COLORADO 80935

The Navigators is an international Christian organi-
zation. Jesus Christ gave His followers the Great
Commission to go and make disciples (Matthew
28:19). The aim of The Navigators is to help fulfill
that commission by multiplying laborers for Christ in
every nation.

NavPress is the publishing ministry of The Navigators.
NavPress publications are tools to help Christians
grow. Although publications alone cannot make disciples or change lives, they can help believers learn
biblical discipleship, and apply what they learn to their
lives and ministries.

Cover illustration: John Martinez

Some of the anecdotal illustrations in this book are
true to life and are included with the permission of the
persons involved. All other illustrations are composites
of real situations, and any resemblance to people living
or dead is coincidental.

Unless otherwise identified, all Scripture in this pub-
lication is from the *Holy Bible: New International Version*
(NIV). Copyright © 1973, 1978, 1984, International Bible
Society. Used by permission of Zondervan Bible Publishers. Other versions used include: the *New American
Standard Bible* (NASB), © The Lockman Foundation 1960,
1962, 1963, 1968, 1971, 1972, 1973, 1975, 1977; and
The Living Bible (TLB), © 1971 owned by assignment
by the Illinois Regional Bank N.A. (as trustee), used
by permission of Tyndale House Publishers, Inc.,
Wheaton, IL 60189.

Printed in the United States of America

Contents

*To the Lord
whose compassions comfort me,
and to Lloyd
whose love and encouragement strengthen me.*

Acknowledgments

I would never have started or finished this book without the Lord's love, healing, wisdom, and courage—which came, to a great extent, through the lives and hearts of others.

Traci Mullins, my editor at NavPress, who first encouraged me to write a book at all, provided welcome encouragement in the process and challenged me to rewrite (from the heart) a key portion. Along the way, she has become a cherished friend.

My friends who read the manuscript in progress and offered invaluable suggestions and encouragement—Debbie Keuer, Judy Robinett Long, Frances "Poosie" Swann, and Cathy Vanderpool.

Nancy Leaverton Hutson, my mother, who has always believed in and encouraged me and my abilities. Her willingness to bless this book, even though my story inevitably involves hers, is a tribute to her faith and love.

Nan Timmons, Laurie Glaske, and Holly Baker—my

sisters who, with their love, music and laughter, formed my earliest "support group" in silent pain.

Friends who prayed faithfully—Marsha Alderson, Zelia McGaha, Loretta VanCleave; and family—my mother-in-law, Ruth Olsen, and sister-in-law, Linda Olsen.

Most of all, my husband, Lloyd, who has cheered this project from the start. He listened keenly to every word on Wednesday afternoons over coffee—just as he listens to my heart as I grow through silent pain. Finally, thank you, Brian and Mark, for often having patience when the door of my study was closed. And bless you, too, for the times you opened it anyway.

PART ONE

HURTING

1

Silent Pain:
A Low-Grade Fever
of the Heart

&.

There is a pain so utter
It swallows Being up,
Then covers the abyss with trance
So memory can step
Around, across, upon it.
EMILY DICKINSON

Life hurts. We may love the streaming pageant with all its people, possibilities, and pleasures, but we cannot escape its emotional pain. Some of the pain grabs our attention and demands resolution. But some part of it can easily be overlooked, discounted, and pushed aside into a dark corner of our souls.

Much of my own spiritual and emotional growth has come as a result of wrestling with this often elusive emotional pain, which twenty years of commitment to Christ is only now eroding. I call it "silent pain."

By silent pain I don't mean the crisis grief that follows the tragedies of our lives. We've all had our share of those, and more will come. Those are loss events that we survive in time, in tears, in faith, in connection with sympathetic friends and families who call us, feed us, hug us, pray for us, and then help us go on.

By silent pain I mean the lingering pain, the sub-

11

merged sadness, the deep ache that we neither feel hourly nor forget for more than a day or two. The deep longings of our hearts that remain unfulfilled and look more out of reach every day.

I mean the disappointments in our relationships with husbands, children, and parents that convince us we will never relate as deeply as we desire to with anyone on earth. Or that gray, uncertain feeling about who we are that we can't quite put a finger on. Those "necessary losses" that we've never been able to face, and those hurts that have never fully healed. In our minds we've forgiven, perhaps even mentally forgotten, but not in our hearts.

So we hush the pain, just like we jostle our restless infants during church to keep them from disturbing others.

This is silent pain.

For many of us, the crises of life are easier to endure than the slow-burning, quiet pains. During crisis, others rush to support us when the flame of disaster is still high. But later, or deeper, or more silent and nagging, are the pains we can't easily explain or justify. The troubles that nobody but Jesus knows, or feels, or wants to hear.

And we often wonder whether He does.

THE FACES OF SILENT PAIN

I recently received a letter from a woman who has known and served the Lord for years. She also has a fulfilling business career and bright future. Yet with candor and precision, she describes a dimmer reality within her soul.

> For me the most frightening and painful thing about life is simply being alive. . . . It has something to do with God's opening up vulnerable parts of me that I don't know what to do with. I am more "alive" than I've ever been in terms of experiencing my own longings and losses, but I experience very little of God's compassion and the bittersweet comfort and

joy that comes from that. Most of the time I feel agonizingly alone in this process.

This is silent pain. Like a parasite, it quietly steals life from its host. Her creative energy and spontaneity wane. Vital connections with loved ones lose their spark in the self-conscious distance between what she feels and what she can express. Hope dwindles in a God who seems untouchable and untouching.

Mary is a thirty-seven-year-old friend with a faithful, supportive Christian husband and four active children. Until recently, hardly a day went by that Mary didn't feel uncomfortable whenever she was alone. She had battled a chronic sense of inadequacy and low self-esteem that her close fellowship with the Lord had never "cured." Although she had faced some of the unresolved conflicts from her past, she couldn't shake the haunting pain that lingered in the present.

Mary had forgiven her dad for abandoning her when she was a little girl. She also forgave and struggled to separate from her mother. Mary realized that her mother had clung so desperately to her when Mary was a child and controlled her so completely in fear of losing her, that Mary had conformed to her mother's needs and lost her God-given identity in the process.

A free spirit lived inside Mary. She longed to be the artist, to live in the country, and to express beauty in every medium she could touch. But her role in childhood, her piece of the vacuum to fill, was that of a dutiful, by-the-book daughter. Her mother couldn't tolerate giving Mary room to be herself.

Norman Wright, Christian counselor and author, describes why we take on childhood roles in the family structure:

> Your role was your mask, your way of coping with the pain of not having your needs fully met by your father and other family members. If you didn't

receive recognition or affirmation for who you were, you took on a role which garnered you the attention you needed.[1]

Mary tried to break free from her dutiful role, but the attempt was painful. She felt inadequate because she thought she would never become the woman she was created to be. She often felt afraid and alone.

This was Mary's silent pain. She was caught between giving up the secure but smothering love of her mother and taking hold of the confidence that a father can give—a father who was never there for Mary. She battled a competency crisis that was harder for her to overcome than for some of her peers, even though she had made the grades and married the good guy. When she struggled more than others, Mary felt a kind of shame that shielded her from God's tender compassion and healing fatherhood. The words of Psalm 103:13, "As a father has compassion on his children, so the LORD has compassion on those who fear him," were only words to Mary.

Eventually, after much prayer and counseling, and through facing her silent pain, Mary began to assert her independence from her mother and embrace her dependence on the Lord. As she experienced intimacy with God as her compassionate Father, Mary began to express herself with more confidence, accept her limitations, and pursue her artistic talents.

❧

Cindy was a vital, talented, middle-aged mother of three. Her busy schedule kept her mind off silent pain most of the time. But when Cindy was alone, or during her quiet time, she sensed a deep emptiness in her heart that Bible study, prayer, and service had never filled. Sometimes music tapped that empty space, and Cindy wept, crying out for something she couldn't identify, like a baby who cries without understanding her hunger.

Cindy sometimes overwhelmed her husband by expecting him to fill this nameless longing. When he couldn't, she felt desperately alone, even as she cried to the God of comfort. Living a life of faithfulness to the Lord and to her responsibilities, Cindy often shoved the distraction of silent pain into a bulging drawer of neglected emotions. But its drain on her energy kept her emotionally unavailable for deeper relationships with her family, Christian friends, and those outside the faith.

Cindy described her family of five as having been stretched and warped by the reality of an alcoholic mother and a father who worked twelve- to fourteen-hour days to build and maintain a successful law practice. Cindy, the second of three daughters, had learned early on to take care of herself, to perform at school for teacher approval, and to give all appearances of having survived without a scratch. But the inner wounds and her attempts to cover them eventually combined to magnify her pain.

While Cindy was in college, her mother committed suicide. Cindy went to a campus ministry seeking a source of friendship and hope. Graciously, the Lord called her to Himself with the good news of Christ's love and redeeming grace through His death and resurrection. Cindy found new life, new hope, and some consolation. But still festering inside her was the deep grief and anger she could not yet feel about her mother, her distant father, and her profound childhood losses.

An older Christian student soon began discipling Cindy, and the two developed a fast friendship. Cindy listened intently as Lynn opened the Scriptures to her in a way she had never heard before. The Holy Spirit gave her truth, love, and grace in such concentrated doses through Lynn that Cindy abandoned herself to her Christian shepherdess, opening her unmet childhood needs to this sensitive spiritual guide.

And together they fell. From the heights of redeeming grace to the depths of sexual immorality, with one decision.

One choice that felt so right, that anesthetized the buried pain—yet deepened the wound at the same time. The confusing relationship lasted six months before Cindy, torn by guilt, finally pulled away.

How did it happen *after* salvation when it had never happened before? Why had it seemed to Cindy like an oasis in the desert but then turned out to be worse than a mirage?

These painful questions plagued Cindy—even after twelve years of marriage to a kind man, the birth of three children, and the spiritual growth of mind and heart that she thought would fill the dark, confusing places within her.

This is another silent pain: the struggle of facing sadness and confusion in the deepest reaches of the soul, because something that should have been filled long ago is empty and our sinful flesh devises damaging ways to fill the void.

Cindy was continuing to experience the brokenness within her. Her inner pain communicated that something was missing in her faithful search to become whole. Something as vital to her soul as food to her body. Something that ten years of prayer, diligent Bible study, and obedience to Christ had not filled.

Silent pain finally succeeded in calling Cindy back to those abandoned, wounded places in her soul. Through prayer, counseling, reading, and others' support, the Lord began to touch Cindy's pain with His compassion and shine light into the dark places. She embraced the Lord as her nurturing Father and affirmed her new identity in Christ. Cindy's marriage deepened and her intimacy with God grew. She had new energy, confidence, and love to risk reaching out.

≈●

These are a few of the faces of silent pain, the submerged sorrow within many women that often hides beneath a calm surface of maturity. The tragedy is that many women don't give themselves permission to feel the pain, or they start to feel it and then try to cover it again in fear of unending depression. That's why the pain becomes silent. This very silence, this reluctance to face the pain, separates these women from vital parts of their souls that have been damaged. Vital parts that the Lord wants to heal and empower with love.

Linda Schierse Leonard describes this problem:

> They feel alienated from their center because they
> are cut off from important parts of themselves. It is
> as though they have a mansion for their home but are
> living in only a few of the rooms.[2]

Opening doors to these forgotten rooms usually involves confronting silent pain.

WHAT IS SILENT PAIN?

Because this silent pain quietly saps our energy, I call it *the low-grade fever of the heart*. But it's a paralyzing disease. We're often tempted to walk on the other side of the road from it, the way we would avoid an infectiously ill person or a dead animal for fear of contamination.

Many Christian teachers have diagnosed this kind of pain as an illness that can be remedied simply by faith. With the same message that is sometimes given to those who are physically ill, they assert that if we haven't gotten better by trusting the promises, then we just "don't have enough faith."

But I can't walk around silent pain anymore. Because I, too, was a victim of it for years—in the knowledge of Scripture, in the context of faith and service, in the midst of the storm, in the quietness of tranquil times.

I can't turn my back on silent pain, because I desire to know intimately this Man who walked in perfect faith yet was described as a "man of sorrows, and familiar with suffering" (Isaiah 53:3). I want to reenter more rooms in my mansion, not live with parts of me quarantined from the Lord, from myself, and from those He wants me to love.

Are you suffering with a feverish heart? I care deeply about you, and I want to help you look beyond the symptom of the pain to the deep hurts that may be infecting your soul. I may not know you here on earth, but the Lord says we are one, you and I—just as He and the Father are one. And we will know each other in heaven.

Are you keeping quiet about the struggles you live with? The Lord Jesus knows you completely, and He wants you to be able to talk about silent pain. Maybe no one has ever given you permission to talk about it, but He has. That's part of what this book opens up to me: a place to speak the truth in love, and to trust Love to speak the truth in you.

I write because I am beginning to see Him better. I long to share with you, and have you share with me, more of what we see as we believe the depth of His compassion, His desire to feel with us in our pain and deliver us through it—especially our silent pain. Until finally, "the kindness of God leads [us] to repentance" (Romans 2:4, NASB): a deep desire to be whole, to be full, to be like the One who groaned, wept, and died for us, and who lives that we may be filled with His joy and pour out His love to others. Until finally, we feel intimately loved by a Father who holds us by the hand and encourages us to be all we can be—not in order to earn His love, but to enjoy Him more deeply in loving and comforting others.

My deepest desire in this book is to comfort those who are in any trouble with the comfort that I have received from God (2 Corinthians 1:4). But as you are all too aware, the work of receiving that comfort from Him is still a private work in your own heart. I want to come alongside, to look together at the Scriptures and ideas that paint a fuller portrait of the emotional, compassion-filled heart of our Father, so that Christ's sympathy for us and for others may be formed in us.

WHAT DOES SILENT PAIN FEEL LIKE?

Silent pain comes wrapped in different packaging. Sometimes it's labeled clearly. But sometimes it's covered in a brown paper that shrouds it in mystery, and we have to shake it and squeeze it to discover its contents. What's tucked inside these wrappings may be too vague or private to describe at prayer meetings. So we toss these packages aside, unopened.

The mysteries of the heart are not easily identified. But I want to describe a few "silent pain packages" I've tossed aside without opening. Perhaps some will be familiar to you.

A grief too deep to describe, or too difficult for others to understand. This silent pain may be residual grief from a past loss or broken relationship that we've never completely resolved. Others may think we should "get over it." But time alone doesn't heal all wounds.

We sense this silent pain when the memory of the event or person (many years past) still brings tears or obvious pain. At the other extreme, we may describe the painful event or relationship with no feelings at all. Our description sounds more like an impersonal news report than the story of a significant personal event.

This residual grief may also stem from the constant strain of caring for an ill or disabled parent, nursing a chronically ill or disabled child, or living with our own long-term health problems. In these trials, it's hard for others to "hang in there" with us over the long haul.

A recurring inner ache that we don't feel free to talk about. This package of silent pain keeps arriving at our heart's door after experiences that are similar to the original crisis—for example, when a friend fails us or an important relationship appears to be in trouble. More than disappointing, these related events feel deeply threatening to our stability and security. Our emotions have been "through this" before, so the present distress is multiplied by all the other painful experiences like it. But because we feel that we're overreacting to something that we "should" be able to handle more maturely, we don't admit our difficulty to others.

A troubled spirit related to unresolved doubts and questions. We may have important unanswered questions, discomfort with accepted Christian practices, or distress over confusing events. But either we can't formulate the question, or, if we do, we can't bring ourselves to ask God directly or take it to a spiritual leader. This uncertainty undermines our intimacy with the Lord, but we're afraid or unable to confront it. We feel alone, and often guilty.

An emotional drain caused by a recurring temptation in our lives. We feel sad or guilty for even being tempted, although we know that temptation is not sin. Jesus Himself was tempted in the same ways we are, the Bible says, yet He was without sin (Hebrews 4:15). Although we may resist or flee evil, we still sense something broken inside us that continues to be vulnerable, and we need someone to talk to about it. Even those who successfully recover from alcoholism, chemical dependency, codependency, or patterns of sexual immorality sometimes experience emotional pain as they resist sin. The constant, long-term nature of the battle — sometimes lifelong — can spawn silent pain.

A numbing sense of guilt or shame over past or present sin, real or imagined. Our souls are locked in torment when we are unable to receive God's cleansing forgiveness at a deep level for the things we do to harm others, Him, or ourselves. We are afraid even to seek His face for fear we will meet His furious stare — or worse, His refusal to look at one so wicked or disgusting. When we are deeply convinced our Father could not possibly welcome us just as we are, we exist submerged in silent pain. We don't dare embrace any of the joys of life or fellowship. And we feel terribly, terribly alone.

A chronic, vague distress over our identity, our role, and our place in God's plan. We want to know who God created us to be and how to fulfill His design for us. We want to be all we can be in Christ. Carol Kent calls this feeling "creative restlessness" and distinguishes it from sinful discontent.[3] Whether you're a homemaker, a career woman, or one who works inside and outside the home, you may feel unheard, unappreciated, stretched too thin, inadequate, insignificant, or all of the above. As women in a changing world, we question our value and feel silent pain over the possibility of not mattering in God's plan.

THE DIFFERENCE BETWEEN PAIN AND LONGING

As I experienced silent pain and listened to others who also endured it, I discovered two things we often had in common: (1) an uncertainty about the validity of our silent pain, and (2) a sense that there was something missing as we tried to move through this pain to comfort and acceptance in the Lord.

It's important to distinguish silent pain from the "groaning" that Scripture says we will always feel this side of heaven (Romans 8:22-23). Dr. Larry Crabb believes that mature Christians will experience a certain level of perpetual sadness until the Lord brings in His Kingdom. But silent pain goes beyond that. As one friend wrote, "I know that the pain I feel is not the groaning the Bible talks about. It's something more destructive."

Our normal longings for heaven are different from this destructive side of silent pain. Spiritual longings are clear, acknowledged, and entrusted to the Lord for future fulfillment. In contrast, silent pain is often hidden, confusing, and responsible for unnecessary suffering or sinful patterns in our life. Silent pain is a little like the discordant music that warns me when to shut my eyes before something unpleasant in a movie. It doesn't *say* anything. It just makes me feel bad and react defensively.

Silent pain is more than a longing. It interferes with our living and our loving.

WHY WE HOLD ON TO THE PAIN

I'm well acquainted with silent pain. Until a few years ago, I often went through times when simply facing the day with energy and hope required a singular act of courage.

Sometimes I felt like a child who had just been left on a street corner, although I was actually standing in a group of friends. It always hurt to face the reality once more that the "perfect relationship" I dreamed would fill all my needs would never happen in this life with anyone I could see and touch.

I often struggled unsuccessfully to determine whether I was feeling true guilt or the natural discomfort that came from not pleasing others, or not achieving enough, or not living up to someone else's standard. Although I had studied God's Word extensively and followed His ways for twenty years, that old, nagging pain constantly erupted, and I was caught again between what I knew and how I felt. And then I felt guilty for feeling what I felt.

Why do Christians, who have every reason to be set free from the trap of their pain, keep wrestling this nameless, untiring foe? I have explored this question for years. Through reading, counseling, and participation in various support groups for chronic pain, both Christian and secular, I have been led to look to the past—not in order to blame, but in order to understand the patterns in my life.

The Need to Explore the Past
Jesus said, "I tell you the truth, unless you change and become like little children, you will never enter the kingdom of heaven" (Matthew 18:3). For me, this return to childlikeness includes, among other things, going back to that vulnerable place in my life when I first began to feel the inevitable pain of living in a fallen world. Since there are no perfect parents—for all of us are limited, sinful, and unable to shield our kids from all pain and suffering—every child will face emotional damage. Some, of course, face more

damage than others, depending on their parents' own inner struggles and outward limitations.

Some children face the effects of severe abuse and intentional offenses. Others must deal with the less obvious, but equally valid, pain from their parents' unintentional neglect. Karen Mains writes, "It is my personal belief that we suffer more [often] from the inadvertent acts than from the deliberate ones. Most people do not know they have hurt us. At any rate . . . the results are the same: pain."[4]

I look back, not to blame others for my adult failures, but to face my own hurts and losses and to learn what sinful defenses I used to shield myself from the pain or to get what I needed from others. Facing these unmet childhood needs with vulnerability, by forsaking self-protective ways, often triggers deep grief. Judith Viorst calls it the grieving of our "necessary losses." This particular grief is the loss of perfect parenting.

Once we face our immature childhood strategies for dealing with pain, we can begin the long process of replacing them with God's ways of handling our pain and filling our deeply-felt, legitimate needs. Jesus seems to be saying that in Him, we are not only born again, but we also get to grow up again.

In his book *Inside Out*, Dr. Larry Crabb encourages Christians to begin this process.[5] He describes how we have been hurt by the sin of others. In the wake of that pain, we have developed self-protective and demanding ways of trying to survive. These habits have become our sin patterns, and they are so much a part of us that we don't recognize them. We are damaged by others, yes. But the sin comes from our own wayward hearts, in response to the pain. Crabb argues that we will never admit the depth of our sin until we can feel just how hurt we have been, and see how important our self-protection has become to us. Only then can we honestly face the pain, trusting God alone to be our provider and defender. Only then can we become genuinely human, vulnerable, loving men and women of God.

We are both victims and agents of sin. As young girls and adult women, we have been wounded by the sin of others. That is our pain. But we have also created defenses against that pain by wounding ourselves and others with overt or subtle patterns of self-protection and self-reliance. That is our sin.

If we struggle with low self-esteem, we may subtly manipulate others to love us by doing nice things for them. If we have been wounded by critical parents, we may quietly demand approval from others by overworking and then resenting all negative feedback. If our fathers didn't give us what we needed, we may transfer those expectations to our husbands and pout when our "requests" go unheeded.

We end up stalled between the pain and the sin, afraid to let go of our defenses and just as afraid not to let go of our sin. We feel alone, vulnerable to being hurt again, and stuck in silent pain because it's so hard to feel that anyone understands how deeply hurt we are, how tender are the broken places inside us, and how much we long for perfect love to make us whole again. We assume we're not permitted to feel the pain, and so we're unable to start the healing process.

One reason we get stuck is that we don't believe and experience enough of the tender compassion and comfort of God, and therefore we don't have compassion on ourselves. We may view God as tolerant of our emotional pain, but not deeply sympathetic. We know that compassion is one of His attributes, but we haven't felt it deeply enough to find true comfort for our silent pain.

I believe that we won't fully be able to let go of our sinful strategies for dealing with pain until we find the intense compassion of Jesus Christ. If He came all the way from heaven and plunged into the depths of hell to save us, then we can trust Him to come all the way into our pain and rescue us with compassion. "We love because he first loved us" (1 John 4:19).

A PERSONAL STORY OF SILENT PAIN

As I look back, one of the defenses that protected me as a child was simply not to feel the pain. I was afraid it would overwhelm me. But as an adult, this defense has interfered with my walk of faith, and I need to choose to let it go. As a child of God, I can now face reality and find true comfort by delving deeper into a precious part of the nature of our Lord—the depths of His compassion.

As one of six children, I grew up in a Christian home. But it was shaped and shaken by the effects of my father's alcoholism. My mother struggled emotionally with the stress of home and teaching school to help support us. After my parents divorced when I was sixteen, my father's emphysema grew worse, and five years later he died of a self-inflicted gunshot wound. In a period of eleven years before and after the divorce, my mother was hospitalized three times for treatment of extreme emotional illness. Through it all, I couldn't talk about my grief or resolve it. So it became silent pain.

A year or so after marrying at age thirty-one, I gave birth to our first child, Brian, who has spina bifida—a major disabling birth defect. For the first eighteen months we had to resuscitate him frequently, because whenever he cried hard, he would stop breathing. Over the first four years, he endured frequent crises and numerous surgeries. The Lord gave us strength to endure, but the physical trauma for Brian and the emotional trauma for us were almost overwhelming. Through God's gracious intervention, Brian is now healthy, though physically disabled, and wheels himself to a regular fourth-grade class.

Brian is a blessing, and in many ways his present trials aren't very different from any other child's. But his hidden struggles with disability at different stages of life still hurt.

Nine years later, I still feel lingering pain—silent pain—over Brian. Sometimes I think my faith should have washed it away by now. But I'm the only one who feels it the way a mother does, and there are very few people to talk to without feeling I have to qualify everything with the assurance that I still trust God. I *do* trust Him to do His will, to show His strength through weakness. Brian's life has encouraged many already. I rejoice in that. But a residual grief has remained which is more than a longing for heaven. It is a sense of brokenness that is now healing as Christ magnifies His compassion in me.

Several years after Brian was born, another tidal wave struck our shores. In 1986, I was diagnosed with multiple sclerosis. My first reaction was shock. For two weeks after the news, I glibly told people how mild the disease would be and how there was nothing to worry about. I even made jokes about it. With my old pattern of suppressing sadness, I rushed past the normal emotion of sorrow.

But it finally dawned on me that the disease meant that I might face a disability as great as our son's, that I might become unable to be the physical help to Brian that he currently needed, that I might have to give up many of the ways I cared for my family and place more burdens on my husband's shoulders. I didn't know the future, and I had to face the awful possibilities with raw faith, not glib optimism. I was shaken to the core.

When I finally let myself feel the pain, and pour it out, the Lord gave me His comfort. During that time of wrestling, He also let me see my pattern of suppressing emotion and how the pattern itself could be contributing to my health problems. Over the next eighteen months, the episodes of physical pain disappeared, and eventually I stopped needing the medication the doctors had prescribed. Gratefully, I am now symptom-free and have a good prognosis.

It took the specter of a nerve-rotting disease to awaken me to the way I was crippling myself with a soul-rotting pattern of emotional repression . . . in the name of faith. Not only my body had suffered, but my marriage had careened on the brink of indifference and deadly neglect. Our two sons trembled when I kicked the kitchen cabinet door so hard it cracked down the middle. I, Kathy Olsen, always known for her gentle, calm spirit, had become a gentle, calm volcano.

But wasn't I strong? Hadn't I ridden the crashing waves of Brian's repeated medical crises? I had resuscitated him hundreds of times when he stopped breathing and never had to resort to tranquilizers. Hadn't I testified of the strength the Lord gave us again and again? Because He certainly did. The Lord fills even broken vessels.

But I had no deep inner peace. Even before my diagnosis, Lloyd and I had already started marriage counseling. I was beginning to discover how sad and mad I really felt under all my public tranquility and image of strong faith. At first, emotions scared me. I had always worked to keep my feelings under control. I felt that if I didn't express those emotions, they wouldn't have control over me.

It was my Damascus Road the day the Lord opened my eyes to two simple truths. First, I learned that *my emotions are neither good nor bad in themselves.* Only my thoughts and actions *in response* to those feelings have moral value. "Be angry," Scripture says, "and yet do not sin" (Ephesians 4:26, NASB). I think the same principle applies to all our negative emotions. Second, and here was the clincher, *my emotions were going to control me indirectly if I didn't face them, feel them, and use their energy wisely.* Therefore, if I buried anger and grief in the name of control, I was fooling myself. Norman Wright explains,

> Repressed feelings cause people to do things they don't intend to do, like yelling at the children, abusing pets. . . . By repressing your feelings, you are no longer in charge of them. You don't know when or where they will pop up.[6]

My dying marriage, angry outbursts, and health problems were the destructive effects of unresolved negative emotions. Why hadn't I seen it before? The graveyard of my buried sorrow and pain was now a haunted basement at the depths of my soul, from which ghosts of loss and grief forayed into the few open rooms of my mansion. I was controlled, distorted, and further grieved by their silent, destructive raids.

Where was the Holy Spirit during all this? Why hadn't He run all these demons out of my dwelling? I have come to believe that *the Lord does not address the depths of our emotional needs until we are ready and we ask Him*. It had taken disease to make me ready.

I sat on my bed one day, agonizing over the depths of emotional pain I was feeling, as if all the ghosts had been loosed at once. I lay prone on the floor, face down, and cried out to the Lord. There didn't seem to be any immediate response from heaven. But now, looking back over the intervening five years, I know that He heard me and answered my despairing cry.

In the days and weeks following that desperate appeal, one of the answers I kept hearing came from Psalm 51:6: "Surely you desire truth in the inner parts; you teach me wisdom in the inmost place." My inmost place felt like a wasteland. Despite all my faith and biblical knowledge, it was desperately wounded, a breeding ground for wild and uncontrolled growth. This ache was more than the "groaning" we all experience until God's Kingdom comes. This was the warning signal of silent pain—an alarm alerting me to the presence of toxic doses of unresolved emotions hidden within.

About all I could say at the time was, "Lord, tell me anything about my inner being You want me to know. Anything. I'm helpless. Please heal me." I took those words from Psalm 51 with me to every counseling session, because I knew no one but the Holy Spirit could counsel me as deeply and effectively. But I also knew I needed human help, and God provided that, too.

I was ready to let go of more of my self-made coping

mechanisms, and that meant getting acquainted with silent pain. I knew that the Lord had introduced us. In fact, *I began to see that silent pain was His still, small voice to call me back into the abandoned rooms of my mansion.* He took me by the hand, it seemed, and walked me into the darkness. I began to sense His presence even in the pain. And He reassured me with His words, "Even the darkness will not be dark to [Me], and the night will shine like the day, for darkness is as light to [Me]" (Psalm 139:12).

RECOGNIZING THE PANGS OF FATHER HUNGER

For many women, trusting God in the dark is particularly difficult because of inadequate, even abusive, "care" from their fathers during childhood. Linda Schierse Leonard begins her book *The Wounded Woman* with this description of women in silent pain:

> Every week wounded women come into my office suffering from a poor self-image, from the inability to form lasting relationships, or from a lack of confidence in their ability to work and function in the world. On the surface these women often appear quite successful — confident businesswomen, contented housewives, carefree students, swinging divorcees. But underneath the veneer of success or contentment is the injured self, the hidden despair, the feelings of loneliness and isolation, the fear of abandonment and rejection, the tears and the rage.[7]

She goes on to explain the thesis of her book: This hidden despair, this deep wound women feel, often stems from a damaged relation with their fathers. Leonard speculates that when a father is damaged in his own psychological development, he is unable to give his daughter the love and guidance she needs.

It's tempting for Christians to dismiss this secular theory with the explanation that these women, many of whom may be nonChristians, didn't have the resource of God's forgiveness for them and the power to forgive their fathers. But that dismissal skates blithely across a surface of thin ice. Norman Wright, author of *Always Daddy's Girl*, confirms that the lack of fathering plagues Christian women as well. Gary Smalley and John Trent agree that there is a "'father hunger' in many women's hearts today . . . these hurtful memories act like sandpaper on a woman's soul."[8]

Wright explains how a woman's emotional development is often damaged by poor father-figures. One of the central functions a father has in his daughter's growth, according to Wright, is influencing her sense of competency. Dad becomes a steppingstone from home into a world that would otherwise seem overwhelming to a young woman. "A father's confidence in his daughter and her capabilities will instill in her the confidence to survive on her own," he writes. "His positive involvement can help his daughter from becoming overly dependent on her mother."[9] Without that positive involvement, women sustain injuries that may turn into lifelong wounds.

A Christian response to these wounds is to seek growth through them rather than to fixate on blaming those who inflicted them. Wright provides helpful insights for how a woman can move toward wholeness in Christ as she works through her pain to emotional reconciliation with her father.

I have been finding such reconciliation with my own father, even though he died twenty years ago. Here was a talented, charming man whom I had once adored, who had suffered alcoholism, disease, and finally suicide because he had never known what to do with his own pain. As he awkwardly parented me and continued to hurt himself, I used the same emotional repression he had used to cut myself off from the hurt—and from him. I'll fill in more of the details of that story later.

In my search for reconciliation with my father, I have discovered another disturbing reality. I've realized that I must come to terms with the same lack of emotional parenting from another patriarchal figure in my life: the churches and church leaders who have shepherded me as a Christian.

Hunger for a Heavenly Father
In addition to earthly father hunger, I believe there is also an unmet "heavenly Father hunger" among many women who have longed for and missed a complete portrait of the personhood of their God. Particularly that part of the portrait—visible in Scripture, but perhaps not translated well by many teachers—which describes the intense emotion and compassion of God the Father and the Lord Jesus Christ.

All of us are imperfect. As groups of imperfect people, many church leaders, pastors, and congregations have unintentionally failed to provide an adequate model for handling emotion—particularly grief, anger, and pain. I understand that they have had little or no modeling in their own training, and therefore I don't blame them. Male leaders can't be expected to empathize with uniquely female emotional needs, because men and women are different by design, and this includes differences in how we handle pain.

As Christian women, we can lovingly accept these human limitations in others and seek the Lord's guidance in this area so vital to our own spiritual growth. We can also take responsibility, by God's grace, for asking, seeking, and knocking until we find in Jesus Christ and His Word the emotional model that we can embrace and pass on to the next generation.

For me, one of the roots of the problem is an incomplete portrait of the compassion of God. This incomplete understanding always results in an incomplete imitation of His character in our lives.

Finding the Emotional Heart of God

The God in whose image we are made feels and expresses His emotions with such fervor that we tremble in their wake. Were we to experience their full power directly, we would melt in the intense heat of His warmth and compassion.

We would abandon ourselves to God in passionate longing to be with Him, to embrace Him, to serve Him—if we could see just how deeply and emotionally He longs for us . . . if we could see the Man of Sorrows weep, the Holy Spirit grieve, and the Father of all comfort tenderly holding his daughter as she cries over her wounds and her own sinful attempts to heal them.

Much, though not all, of that side of our holy God has been hidden too long. Or it has been described in metaphors or images that don't touch our hearts at the deepest level. We need to accept our responsibility to search out the exquisite garden of God's emotion and compassion and find the place of healing for our silent pain.

I encourage you to continue this search until your own pain leads you to the living Bread that alone will satisfy your pangs of father hunger. Please recognize that *emotional pain is not the focus of this book. It is the means to the true focus: the compassion of the Lord Jesus Christ and God our Father.* I pray that our time together in this book may magnify, enlarge, beautify, and praise the compassion of the Lord, so that we can validate our silent pain over nagging losses and longings and experience God's warmth and light in those dark rooms of our soul.

There is a wondrous garden of His compassion just at the end of the path that begins here—here, at your willingness to face silent pain. Maybe you've never truly seen how beautiful this garden can be—but you've heard of it, and by His Spirit and truth, your eyes can also see it. We can move along this path from hurting to healing to helping others by His gracious sympathy and tender power. *But we will have compassion for others only to the degree that we experience Christ's compassion for ourselves.*

We *can* recover from the disabling effects of silent pain, although we know we won't be delivered from hurt forever. Not until we arrive in heaven. Taking our hidden hurts into the heart of God's compassion only means that the pain we feel can become a more positive energy within us, rather than a negative drain. We can experience comfort and a deeper wholeness through opening our innermost being to the One who knows us to the depths of our soul and cherishes us like no other. We can begin to live again in those long-abandoned rooms of our mansion.

When we continue along this path, we will grow to love God more, to love our husbands, children, and friends in a more full-hearted way. We will stop the drain of our God-given emotional energy in silent pain and redirect it to reach a hurting world. We experience freedom to live more joyfully, spontaneously, and lavishly in the service of our best and dearest Friend.

We can walk together down that path to the exquisite garden of God's compassion. As we do, we'll look at the obstacles that have kept us from taking the path sooner. First we need to examine the influences that have been tossing those obstacles across the path: the pressures toward emotional numbness in our culture, in the church, and in ourselves.

2

Why the Pain
Won't Go Away

ॐ

Give sorrow words;
the grief that does not speak
Whispers the o'er-fraught heart
and bids 't break.

SHAKESPEARE, *MEASURE FOR MEASURE*

On a gray February morning seven years ago, Lloyd had left for work, and I had just settled down to another day of being a mother to Brian, then two years old . . . and a waterbed and breakfast to Mark, who wouldn't be born until June.

Through the winter Brian's medical condition had grown steadily worse. His brainstem malformation, which had already required one operation, was now causing him problems with swallowing. He still had apnea (cessation of breathing) when he cried, but now he would start breathing again on his own, rather than having to be resuscitated. With this new swallowing problem, Brian often had a pool of fluid in the back of his throat that would sit there, unable to go either way. The danger was that, if he cried and had an apnea spell, he could aspirate the fluid while he was gasping or unconscious. That could mean pneumonia, which was the *last* thing he needed.

This particular morning Brian and I were in the living room playing on the floor when he started crying and had a "spell." I reached for the syringe to suction the fluid out of his throat. But this time it didn't work. As Brian lay on his back—his skin blue and his body tense—I squeezed the syringe, placed the tip at the back of his throat, then let go. Nothing happened. It wouldn't draw up the fluid.

I was angry and wanted to scream because I felt so helpless and distressed. Thankfully, Brian didn't aspirate, and he came through fine. But it was as if two years of fear, frustration, and anger funneled into that moment, and I experienced an inner explosion, like an atomic bomb detonated underground—violent, but apparently harmless.

It wasn't until years later that I could describe my feelings about that morning. As I had knelt beside Brian, I saw our easy chair across the living room. I realized that if Jesus had been visible and sitting in that chair while all this was happening with Brian, I would have taken the bulb syringe and thrown it at Him!

When I told this story to a group of Christian women last year, just as I made that last statement I heard an audible gasp from the audience.

I understood. Nothing in my background, neither family nor church, would ever have allowed me to acknowledge that kind of anger at God, much less express it. And nothing inside me that awful morning would allow me, because I chose to believe and act out the influences of my training—influences that have been, in most cases, good and healthy blessings in my life. But in this crisis of feeling, I was lacking. I had no idea what to do with wild feelings that came without bidding, despite all that I knew I believed. So I forgot them—at least for a while.

EMOTIONS: THE NEGLECTED CORNER OF THE SOUL

During those several years of Brian's intense medical problems, I repeatedly drew on God's Word in order to escape despair. With my *mind*, I recalled many times the Lord had worked through pain to redeem His people. I recalled the promises that His loving sovereignty would someday trans-form all this suffering—both ours and Brian's—even though we couldn't understand it now. With my *will*, I clung to the call to faithfulness and trust in the midst of pain. "Shall we accept good from God," I repeated with Job, "and not trouble?" (Job 2:10).

So, because the Lord had strengthened my mind with truth and established my will by the power of His Spirit within, I thought that was all I could hope for. But I later realized that the remaining one-third of my soul, my *emotions*, had been off in a far corner, neglected in the clamor to survive the daily demands of caring for Brian. I knew instinctively that I was hurting deeply, but I didn't know how to handle the power of those conflicting emotions *inside* the bounds of faith.

As a result, I grew silently bitter toward God without being aware of it. I continued going to church, having quiet times, being "faithful." Often, when asked what I was learn-ing during those difficult days, I would reply, "That God is God." Which was another way of saying, "He's bigger than I am, and I'm resigned to that fact." I felt like Peter when Jesus questioned whether the disciple would leave Him as other followers had. "Lord," Peter shrugged, "to whom shall we go? You have the words of eternal life" (John 6:68).

I knew I had no sensible choice except to trust Him, but I also thought I had no emotional choice but to bury my enormous pain. I was afraid to feel all my grief and the anger that might come with it.

Only later did I uncover the deepest passion of my heart during those days. I didn't have many questions about God's sovereignty or my duty. I knew the Scripture well enough to have all the "answers" I could expect about those issues. My deepest question didn't involve the mind or even the will.

My questioning cry, so obscured by pain that I could barely hear it, was, *Lord, how do You feel about this?* Close behind was the corollary, *How should I feel about this?*

But I didn't ask, seek, and knock. Sure, I knew that Jesus could "sympathize with our weaknesses" (Hebrews 4:15) and that He "carried our sorrows" (Isaiah 53:4)—but that knowledge really didn't mean very much. It didn't translate well into a soul like mine that was so programmed to deny deep emotion.

In time, God's mercy brought outward relief. The Lord began to heal Brian. After years of life-threatening complications, he began to go days, then weeks, then months between apnea spells. At three years old he came through the last surgery on his brainstem and endured a long recovery. We haven't faced another related crisis since.

But the healing of Brian's body didn't suddenly heal the conflict that had raged inside me. Two realities battled within. On one hand, when God eventually rescued Brian's life, even though he was disabled, I could only be thankful. I praised the Lord that the trauma had passed and that Brian was talking, singing, and enjoying life.

On the other hand, a deep hurt remained unresolved. But how could I complain now?

THE STILL, SMALL VOICE

I chose to keep my anger at God hidden in a storage room of my soul, somewhere down a long hall, beyond the shrill beep of the apnea alarm we still strapped on Brian's chest every night. I suppose I thought that time and thankfulness would heal all wounds. So I stayed in that denial for five years, and could have stayed in it forever, except for one thing.

Silent pain.

And that's why I now hear silent pain as the still, small voice of God. He lives in the mansion of my soul. He knows every nook and corner, because He fashioned me. He doesn't forget the dark, closed-off rooms where someone once lived. He hasn't abandoned the wounded, warped places in my soul—which He created for love—and He doesn't want me to abandon them either.

How Will We Answer?

I tell this story as a way to begin talking about why we get stuck in silent pain. *I'm convinced that our lingering emotional distress isn't caused by the painful events of our lives. It is caused by our silence about those events and the feelings associated with them.* True, many of our families couldn't talk about feelings openly, and we kids learned to hide our feelings, too. But as an adult, I am now responsible to be a better steward of those God-given emotions.

I have learned to answer the still, small voice of silent pain by accepting responsibility for choosing to hide my angry feelings over the crisis with Brian. I am responsible for choosing to ignore the silent pain that simmered long after the crisis pain was over.

But this admission doesn't make me feel guilty. It brings me hope, because I am not a victim. I can, by the grace of God, change the situation. I can let go of silent pain.

That's one of the starting points for the healing power of silent pain: the willingness to face and feel negative emotions left over after a past crisis. Most of us have faced at least one. Yours will be different from mine, but no less painful. Your crisis may have been a profound loss or chronic grief—death in the family, divorce, disability or serious illness, addiction of a family member, career failure. You may have suffered a traumatic experience that allowed fear and anger to penetrate to a deep level of your soul—rape, abandonment, accident, childhood abuse. Or the crisis may have been a "big sin" in your past that planted guilt at such a depth that it is extremely difficult to uproot—such as cruelty, sexual immorality, abortion.

For me the crises were times of anger, frustration, or confusion. But I ignored the pain. Sometimes my anger was masked by mild depression, by feeling "hurt," or by compulsive eating or over-achieving. Later, as a Christian,

I began consciously to forgive others, to accept forgiveness from the Lord, and to trust Him to "work all things together for good" (Romans 8:28). But the pain didn't completely disappear, because my anger, grief, or guilt hadn't been faced and resolved.

I didn't know the sane and simple wisdom that Carol Kent describes in her book *Secret Passions of the Christian Woman*. When she had to go back and sort through her own anger over her miscarriage, she learned that her first angry feelings over disappointment were not sinful:

> The initial anger would not have become sin if I'd had a God-honoring ruling passion (to be totally transparent and honest with Him, committed to working *through* my feelings rather than allowing my anger to grow by pretending it wasn't there).[1]

But before I could face my negative feelings, I suffered years of silent pain. Then I spent years letting God change my mind about those "initial" emotions of deep grief and anger. I hadn't understood that those early feelings were normal, and that Jesus felt sympathy for my pain. By not receiving that divine compassion to hold me close, my anger had become resentment toward God, and my grief had bordered on despair. And this brings me back to our question about why we get stuck in silent pain. Stuck feeling, but not healing.

One central reason I failed in the past to work through those initial negative feelings to resolution is because I didn't thoroughly believe and enjoy the intensely personal compassion of Jesus Christ. I hadn't realized that He has already entered with us into our pain (as well as our sin) in order to rescue us emotionally.

Jeremiah, the prophet who wept (in faith) for years over a dying nation, survived because he rested his sanity on this truth: God's compassion (His suffering *with* me) never fails (Lamentations 3:22). Thus, when he says, "Since my people are crushed, I am crushed," we hear the cry from the heart of Jesus Christ (Jeremiah 8:21).

BLAST, BURY, OR BUILD

It's important to understand what it means to "work through negative feelings" or "enter the pain." This lesson was vital to me. As long as I thought these phrases meant always saying everything I thought and loudly proclaiming my every urge to others in the name of honesty, I couldn't accept it.

Acceptance only came as I learned that I have three basic choices about how to handle strong emotions. I can *blast* others with them, I can *bury* them, or I can use them to *build* better relationships with God, myself, and others.

Blasting Others
One way to express negative feelings is to blast others with our rage, self-pity, or resentment. It's easy to see why this method is called "explosion," because the force of such emotion is directed outward. Many Christians see that blasting others with their strong emotion is unloving. Proverbs warns us about the person who is chronically angry or has outbursts of temper.

Burying Our Feelings
A second way to deal with negative feelings is to bury them by denying that we feel them. Some psychologists call this "implosion," because the damage done is internal. Depression has been defined as anger turned inward on ourselves. Many Christians choose this method because it appears to be less damaging to others.

Building Relationships
The third way of working through negative feelings is based on the belief that emotion is the God-given energy to act or,

if necessary, to change. This allows us to accept our spontaneous feelings in the presence of a compassionate Savior, to express them to Him honestly, and to let Him direct their energy along the path of wisdom (which may or may not include speaking to others).

These definitions are important, because as long as we think of experiencing silent pain as something harmful or unloving, we will resist facing it. Then when we're forced to face it, we can easily get bogged down if we lose the confidence that our buried pain needs to be uncovered, that it is constructive, and that we will be folded in the arms of God's compassion.

So why, even when we know that accepting our emotional distress is constructive, do we often get stuck in it, seemingly unable to achieve any final resolution for it?

For me, the answer was easy and hard all at the same time. The easy part was realizing that the influences on my choice to bury my silent pain in the first place are the same ones that can keep me stuck *feeling* rather than *healing*. The hard part was in looking closely at these influences and recommitting myself to resisting the old ways and continuing in this new path of life.

PRESSURES TO IGNORE THE PAIN

The forces that help us create and sustain silent pain are like the giants in the Promised Land of spiritual and emotional growth. They're heavyweights! If we enter this spiritual battle for deep change with only enough faith to handle six-foot soldiers, what will we do when we meet Goliath and his brothers?

Easy: freeze, reconsider, or retreat. If I don't realize the true proportions of this giant I'm facing, I'll tremble in fear every time his kneecaps show up in my face. When I hear Christians say "just forgive and forget," or when I don't get encouragement to persevere, or when I feel confusion instead of progress, I'll want to quit.

Not so easy now. The pain is no longer silent. It's screaming at me. I'm sitting in a no-man's-land with javelins landing all around me! Throwing out giants in my life that have been entrenched in this land for generations is no walk in the park, even with the whole armor of God.

When I finally pled with the Lord to search my heart and reveal my "anxious thoughts" (Psalm 139:23), I found three major influences on my choice to silence my emotional pain. In one form or another these factors can keep me stuck. Two are internal forces; one is external. The first is *fear*—fear of being overwhelmed, being unwise, and being unloving. These fears are connected to the second negative force: *false messages about handling negative emotions*. Although I have received many truths from my culture, church, and family, I have also received false messages that encourage me to bury my negative feelings (or blast others) rather than deal with them in an honest, responsible way. The third force, an external pressure, is *the feeling of shame*. Dan Allender, Christian psychologist and author, defines shame as "the subjective experience of being exposed as naked. The origin of shame is rooted in our fear of exposure before another."[2] Facing responsibility for our own emotions exposes us to ourselves and sometimes to others.

The Pressure from Fear

One of my deepest fears about entering silent pain and beginning to feel the quietly destructive emotions that raged inside me was the fear of being overwhelmed. The fear of losing control if I ever walked into one of those dark rooms of my soul.

In the past I had seen some who fell apart when they wept with grief or exploded in anger. When they "felt their feelings" it seemed more like the end of the world than a constructive process. I didn't learn how to feel deeply, then work my way through the pain, and consequently realize that strong emotion is a process we can survive and even grow through. Deep emotion appeared to stir up a storm that was more frightening than helpful. So the idea of choosing to feel the pain beneath my polished veneer frightened me, as well.

Christian psychologist and counselor Dr. Sandra D. Wilson describes this fear of strong emotion in adults who have grown up in alcoholic homes (it has been shown that this characteristic develops in other kinds of dysfunctional families as well):

> [Adult] children of alcoholics experience feelings not so much as an inconvenience but as a threat. Old, childhood fear is involved. This is not the strong emotion or feeling of fear, but the fear of feeling a strong emotion. Counselors need to understand that feelings are perceived as dangerous by many adults raised in alcoholic homes.[3]

My fear of strong emotion had quietly buried my anger, grief, and guilt, but silent pain now created a deeper fear — a fear of the storm in my marriage and family. I often wanted to run from my sons' needs rather than satisfy them. My husband and I were polite but not communicating, and I frequently felt distant and hostile toward him. As the storm of internal pain began to build, I was driven to my knees to plead with God for help, deeply desiring "wisdom in the inmost place." Feeling more helpless and dependent than I ever had in my life, I asked the Lord to let me feel, learn, and grow through the pain.

That willingness five years ago to follow the Lord into the dark, abandoned rooms of my soul was somewhat like the choice the Israelites faced as they stood near the Promised Land, trying to decide if they would obey the Lord and enter in. By majority vote, they said no. Their reason? Fear. They had believed the frightening reports by the ten unfaithful spies who said, "The land we explored devours those living in it. All the people we saw there are of great size" (Numbers 13:32).

My fear of being overwhelmed was like a giant in the land. But the Lord had convinced me this was the path. So now my job was to give this fear to Him, which meant that I had to admit and accept how helpless I was to control what would happen. Trust, I'm learning, requires giving up my demand to be in control. And I knew my emotions didn't have to take control, either. A wise and dear friend gave me an invaluable truth when she said, "Your emotions are not who you are. They are something you have." Who I am is a new creature in Christ. Old things are passing away.

My next fear was the fear of suffering spiritual damage. I had a non-specific dread about walking directly into the emotional jungle that had overtaken those dark, neglected rooms of my mansion. Voices from past spiritual training and old failures cried out warnings about being led astray by fickle feelings, and they pushed me back like a strong wind.

There also have been recent books and articles by Christians that caution believers about the snares of psychological healing and other methods of emotional therapy. Those, too, frightened me with their warnings about the New Age movement and occult influences. So the voices of the past were still speaking in the present.

Then there were the warnings about not blaming others for our problems, about the danger of anger at God, and about the doubt and fear that might creep through the cracks of my emotional vulnerability. And all of these giants are certainly out there ready to "give [my] flesh to the birds" (1 Samuel 17:44). To deny that any of them could injure me is prideful indeed.

Therefore, I won't argue with these warnings. I simply testify that the Lord is leading me through. I can say with the formerly disabled man, "I was blind but now I see" (John 9:25). I don't believe that anyone who knows the Lord and His Word, who asks Him to work in her inner being, and who entrusts herself to the care of a loving Father will be fed to the vultures. Yes, "be of sober spirit, be on the alert"

(1 Peter 5:8, NASB). But don't let fear of the spiritual battle keep you paralyzed on the sidelines.

What most helped me to defeat this giant was to keep reading the Scripture alongside the other books I was reading. I read through the Bible twice in two years. As I did, I saw its truths reflected in and deepened by the new things I was learning about emotions and repentance from old patterns of relationships. And as I read, whatever was *not* true in the other books became more clear.

Another important factor was staying accountable to my husband, to a group of Christian friends, and always to the Lord in prayer. But I have never regretted my decision. In fact, *not* following the Lord's leading in this direction would have been the most spiritually damaging thing I could have done.

When Lloyd and I first talked about seeking counseling, in addition to being wary of unwise council, he was uncertain what might happen to our relationship if we began tracing the source of our troubles. That hesitation, we learned, was based on the third fear that pressures us to ignore silent pain: *the fear of hurting or losing those we love.* Especially if we have established a pattern of burying pain, we fear what might happen if we admit how angry, sad, or fearful we are. We avoid saying anything that may "make" others angry, sad, or fearful. Or perhaps someone we have loved became violent, abusive, or "crazy" when we attempted honest communication, and so we don't want to provoke that kind of response again.

The very practical answer to this fear dawned on me slowly. I began to see that *not dealing with silent pain was already hurting those I loved.* I began to recognize and acknowledge my dishonesty, my unexplainable outbursts, my inability to feel affection, my subtle ways of avoiding intimacy, and my more subtle ways of violating love.

In these situations, we may keep a pretense of right action, but the spirit knows better. Silent pain is a quiet, long-term erosion of the soil of our souls, which saps its nutrients and destroys its life-giving ability. I personally think that long-neglected silent pain is the cause of many failed marriages, especially among Christians.

If our true desire is to grow in our ability to love through fighting these emotional battles of the soul, then the Lord will fight for us. We needn't fear the giants. We can look forward to the land of better spiritual and emotional health. As Joshua and Caleb encouraged the people, "The land we passed through and explored is exceedingly good. If the LORD is pleased with us, he will lead us into that land . . . and will give it to us" (Numbers 14:7-8).

But having faith to fight these three fears necessarily involves the thoughts and beliefs surrounding them. I'm learning that what I think directly affects how I feel. So I began to look again at some false messages I was still believing, which were preventing me from getting through silent pain to a settled peace.

The Pressure from False Messages

False messages from my culture, church, and family background about expressing feelings fed my fears about dealing directly with emotion. These messages are particularly difficult to sort through, because in the right context they are true, not false. They are true *if they refer to irresponsible expressions of emotion.* The are false only when they are used to resist responsible ways of feeling and dealing with negative emotional energy.

Following are four messages that in my experience are most often responsible for sending out false information about dealing with emotion. I don't intend the list to be comprehensive, but simply to give you a starting point for thinking through and discussing with others the kinds of false messages you may have absorbed.

False Message 1: Feeling or expressing negative feelings is not rational, because reason should dominate emotion. At a Christian workshop last year, I was browsing through the book tables when I picked up a small, unimpressive paper-back. The author was familiar to me, but not the title: *The Gift of Feeling*, by Dr. Paul Tournier, a Swiss psychiatrist and devout Christian.

Dr. Tournier describes how the last four hundred years of Western civilization since the Renaissance have consistently exalted human reason and "the sense of things" above emotion and "the sense of the person." As a scholar, Tournier certainly doesn't devalue reason, but he observes an undesirable imbalance between mind and emotion in Western culture. He maintains that reason and objectivity are the aspects of God's character *most* (not exclusively) reflected in men as a group; emotion and intuition are *most* (not exclusively) reflected in women as a group. Both are vital to healthy culture; neither ought to dominate.

Since the Renaissance, Dr. Tournier argues, rationalism has dominated Western culture to its own detriment. With Descartes' "I think, therefore I am," human reason was enthroned. Interestingly, Tournier then draws a historical parallel between the suppression of emotion, intuition, and personalness with the corresponding suppression of women's influence in public life:

> A kind of repression took place: the repression of affectivity, of sensitivity, of the emotions, of tenderness, of kindness, of respect for others, of personal relationship, of mystical communion—and of woman, with whom all the terms in this list are linked by spontaneous association of ideas. Such is our modern Western world, advanced, powerful, efficient, but cold, hard, and tedious.[4]

Although Christianity has had a tempering effect on this trend, the masculine qualities still predominate in public life, according to Tournier. An example of this dominance is that many feminists who wanted to make their mark had to become more masculine in order to do it. Because public life rewarded the masculine strengths of reason, objectivity, and impersonalness, women often imitated men rather than being themselves. Unfortunately, women left behind the feminine essence they appeared to be fighting for, rather than bringing it to bear on a culture in need of it.

The masculinizing influence of rationalism on society remains today, and Tournier sees the differing effects it has on men and women:

> Men find themselves at home in this rational society; they are scarcely even aware of what it lacks. Women, on the other hand, experience a vague unease. Their emotional life and their need of personal contact are left unsatisfied.[5]

Tournier's compassion for the woman's position is articulate and sensitive, but he doesn't assign blame to men and victim status to women. In fact, he calls on women to let their unique expressions of the image of God have more impact on public life. Referring to the impersonality of society, he challenges women: "Instead of suffering from it, they could transform it."[6]

So what does all this have to do with my silent pain that won't go away? For me, this historical awareness helps me see why I don't get the positive feedback about my emotional growth that I want from the world around me. It helps me understand the men I know and the powerful influences that shape them and their world. It helps me, by God's grace, not to take the world's resistance to my emotional and spiritual growth personally. When I am tempted to go back to the old ways of suppressing silent pain—tempted to be "conformed to this world" (Romans 12:2)—I can resist it by faith.

The strong message from the world that tells me to be apologetic for being "emotional," or for handling my feelings responsibly, is certainly one huge, scary giant. But as I learn the wise methods and the spiritual benefits of honestly feeling and expressing my negative *and* positive emotions, God knocks this Goliath of worldly conformity down to size.

False Message 2: Feeling or expressing negative feelings is not spiritual, because faith should dominate emotion. The pressure from this second false message is even tougher to wrestle with. It is the perhaps unintentional signal from some Christians that dealing with negative emotions isn't really necessary for spirituality.

As I have experienced it, the evangelical/fundamentalist model of handling emotion tends to play down the importance of our feelings. I have heard repeated exhortations not to heed our emotions, but rather to listen to the Word and reason. "Don't be too sad, because all things work together for good. Rejoice in everything, since God is sovereign." "This funeral is a celebration," I hear too often, and I wonder how the family member, who will face a year or two of agonizing pain, feels about that. All of these words are true, but when they are repeated over and over without giving equal time to "Blessed are those who mourn" and "Be angry, but do not sin," they become half-truths.

As I listen to others, I sense that one of the main objections some Christians have to "psychological growth" comes when they see friends or relatives begin to feel their pain about the past, or even the present, and then seem to get stuck in it. The person appears to be getting worse rather than better. This is proof enough, they believe, that the process itself is flawed. And I can understand their fears to a degree. We don't want to see loved ones hurt or led astray.

But if we look more closely at the objection—that some people don't benefit from this process—we might find several possible explanations. One explanation may be that the process is biblical, but the person hasn't been faithful to accept her own responsibility for her sinful patterns in response to the pain of the past.

Another possible explanation of apparently unhealthy byproducts is that the person is in the process of feeling the deep disappointment and has gotten sidetracked by blame, but will eventually respond to the Holy Spirit's prompting to let go of blame and find healing. She may need more time and patient support.

Yet another reason may be that the observer is seeing evidence of the struggle but can't interpret it accurately. In other words, her friend may appear to be doing worse, but still be "on schedule" in God's timing. We can't always know what God is doing on the inside of another person. At first, remodeling a house can look like demolition. Sometimes the only way to tell the difference is to wait and see how it turns out.

One obstacle that kept me from entering silent pain sooner was my awareness that I couldn't control the speed of the process. We Christians aren't immune to the cultural pressure to want to cure every ill overnight. We want fast food, fast-acting pain relievers, and three quick steps to emotional healing. If it doesn't work quickly and effectively, then it must not be the Lord's best plan, we reason. Or if we're not healed right away, we assume we just don't have enough faith.

The truth is that it takes courage, faith, and patience to face our pain with integrity. Courage to face the pain and our powerlessness to control the process. Faith and patience to believe that God will see us through if we take responsibility to fight our sinful tendency to demand that our needs be met our way.

"Blessed are those who mourn," declared Jesus, "for they shall be comforted" (Matthew 5:4). One of the blessings of mourning our wounds is that only then can we receive the wealth of compassion God offers. We can't find comfort until we have mourned. Another blessing is that we can learn loving ways of responding to the hurt that we hadn't known before. I couldn't have loved God and others with emotional integrity until I had been comforted. And I couldn't be comforted until I had mourned (given up on) my harmful ways of covering the pain.

Donald W. McCullough explains why he thinks those who mourn the damage that life inflicts deserve our blessing:

> Why are they the blessed ones? How could anyone consider them worthy of congratulation? The first and obvious thing we can say about mourners is that they have enough sensitivity to hurt. That, in itself, deserves praise.[7]

My experience has been that if I don't feel acceptable with my full-blown grief over obvious crisis, then how will I feel accepted if I share a deeper, more vague sadness? And because I have sinned by continuing this false model of emotional repression in myself, my own inner voices keep telling me that I can't really take my silent pain to the Lord. I have sinned because I am hiding from God instead of honestly facing the pain and the challenge of trusting Him with it. Whether stifled by inner or outer restraints, either way I don't feel free to talk about it.

Rather than being quick to judge those who must wade through the messy process of mourning and resolving old wounds—a frequent source of silent pain—perhaps we can affirm their courage to face the battle.

Sadly, if we don't support them, we may be unintentionally playing the role of the ten spies who disheartened the Israelites as they stood just outside the Promised Land. By giving such a fearful report of the size of the giants in the land of milk and honey, we may discourage our brothers and sisters from ever crossing the Jordan of their silent pain.

The decision that faced the Israelites at the edge of the Jordan is the same one I faced before I entered silent pain. It's the same one I face when I get bogged down in the battle. Do I have enough faith to plow ahead? Is this the spiritual course, or is it a path to destruction?

Ultimately, the answers reflect a personal decision, bathed in prayer, for each believer as she seeks the Lord's guidance.

False Message 3: Feeling or expressing negative feelings is not loving, because it disrupts relationship. As we look at the influences on our personal choice to suppress silent pain, I find that the influence of the family, especially the Christian family, is often to silence negative feelings in the name of love.

The message I believed was that any honest expression of anger or disappointment in relationships was unloving because it would disrupt the relationship. That fed the fear that kept Lloyd and me away from counseling for a time. Better to cover the unpleasant feeling and keep the pseudo-peace, I thought, than to uncover it and hurt others.

If those were the only two options, I agree with my family's choice to take the quieter road. I also understand that thirty years ago there was much less information from the church about these issues than there is today. Given the apparently limited choices for handling powerful emotions, the outwardly peaceful route seemed more loving.

But as we grow in psychological awareness, we become more responsible for the wisdom the Lord has given us through His people. With this wisdom, verses such as, "In your anger, do not sin," "speaking the truth in love," and "weep with those who weep" resonate with more depth. This new awareness makes me more accountable for the light I've been given on emotional growth and helps me to avoid becoming judgmental about the limitations of my parents and their generation.

As I learn responsible ways of letting the energy of negative emotions build my ability to love others in grace and truth, I put aside the false message that those feelings will always disrupt relationships. Expressing unpleasant feelings, if that is necessary, doesn't have to mean blasting people I love. Instead, it can mean blessing—greater honesty and intimacy—for our relationships.

False Message 4: Feeling or expressing negative emotions is not practical, because it disrupts our functioning. As you read through the following statements, note how many of them you have said to yourself (or thought to yourself, even if it wasn't in these exact words):

1. I don't have time to feel sad right now. There's too much to do.
2. Yes, I'm angry, but I can't tell her or it would interfere with our project.
3. I probably feel some resentment, but if I think about that I'll never get anything done.
4. This is an emergency. I've got to do my job. Feelings just get in the way, so the best thing to do is ignore them.
5. We'll never figure out this problem if we get bogged down in feelings. Let's just deal with the facts.

The false message that working through emotions is not productive comes from all three of these external influences on our choice to silence pain: the world, the church, and some of our families. In one way or another, all of them can communicate that feeling or expressing negative emotions is not practical. It's not efficient. It doesn't contribute to getting things to run smoothly, to accomplishing the task, or to producing the most.

And there certainly are times when indulging our sorrow, fear, or anger is not appropriate or helpful. Whenever I had to resuscitate Brian, I couldn't afford to engage all my grief or I wouldn't have been able to help him. As I listened to the dramatic reports during the first Allied air strikes on Baghdad in the Persian Gulf conflict, I marveled at how tightly those pilots had to keep a rein on their fear in order to fly through the lethal fireworks of Iraqi antiaircraft artillery.

Doing the best job sometimes requires that we delay processing our emotions. But I falsely concluded that I never needed to go back and take responsibility for that emotional energy I had stored. As a result, the energy went underground and started its malevolent work of undermining my peace and my performance. It has taken me a long time to realize that *repressing emotions is always impractical*, because it will damage my long-term ability to function well.

That functional damage happened to me four years ago when I faced deep emotional struggles, partly because of my inability to work through the powerful feelings I experienced with Brian's disability. As long as I was dishonest with God about my anger toward Him, I couldn't resolve the anxiety that often drove me to be over-protective or over-controlling of Brian—both of which were counterproductive in his life and mine.

By far the most practical benefit of dealing squarely with our feelings in the presence of God is the way it can deepen our relationship with Him. We experience more of His compassion as He tenderly hears and sympathizes with our pain. We take away the power of buried anger or grief, which so often feeds our impractical compulsions to eat, drink, work, protect, or love "too much."

Only then am I free to be a true bond-servant of Christ. Only then am I truly "efficient" in the Kingdom of God.

THE STAYING POWER OF SHAME

One of the most powerful emotions for the woman in silent pain is shame—the feeling of being exposed and utterly unlovable.

When we feel shame, we don't necessarily feel like nobodies all the time. We may even be active and well-rounded. The problem of shame is present when we have a low-level, chronic sense of uneasiness around others. We may be anxious to impress (and therefore succeed). We may apologize often, or for things we didn't cause. (I found myself saying "I'm sorry" when another person lost something or didn't get what she wanted.) We may think we're always imposing on other people when we truly aren't. We may not ever feel okay about asking for help. Or we may feel the need for constant affirmation from others in order to feel good about ourselves.

This general sense of being "less than" relates to our inability to feel our true feelings and get through the process of healing. In simple terms, we don't respect and care wisely for our own feelings. But deep within, we realize we have devalued ourselves. We have denied our own God-given energy and spontaneity, and we experience a mild depression. As David E. Carlson writes,

> Depression often results when a person is not free to experience the very earliest feelings, such as fright, anger, sadness, discontent, pain, hunger, or loneliness, without being rejected, ridiculed, or punished.[8]

As a result, Carlson reports,

> Christian counselees typically evaluate negative feelings as wrong, sinful, immoral, or a measure of their worthlessness. Self-condemnation prevents them from exploring the source and meaning of their feelings and frustrates their completing the process. Prejudging feelings inhibits processing and leads to self-hate (lowered self-esteem) . . . rather than to confession, repentance, and restoration.[9]

Dr. Carlson pinpoints the reason why shame keeps us stuck in the first step of the healing process: *We remain convinced that our feelings themselves are bad.* We still have trouble accepting them, and if *we* can't accept them, then we can't believe and feel Christ's tender compassion for our pain, either.

Shame made me want to hide in order to avoid the pain of exposure. Rather than pouring out my heart to the Lord just as it was (as David did often in the Psalms), I would hide and pretend, thinking I could avoid the pain. It's a vicious cycle: In order to feel less pain, I numbed my feelings . . . which in turn fueled my shame . . . which produced more pain. My strategy backfired!

Our self-made defenses don't really shield us from pain. They only block the front door of our house, while the pain steals its way through the window. But there is a way out of this crazy cycle. And we'll talk more about shame in a later chapter. But to begin, we need a person we can go to who will show us what it means to be emotionally nurtured, before our feelings sour into sin.

FINDING RELIEF FROM SHAME AND ANGER

We need someone who will embrace us even in our shame. Someone who, even when we feel embarrassed for being needy, will put his arms around us, hold us gently and long, reassuring us that he understands why we're tempted to retreat. Then he will tell us not to be afraid of our feelings, because he is here—will always be here—to listen *without condemning*.

Maybe then, if we believe him, our painful feelings will peek around the corner again, like a shy child who has waited until everyone's gone. And we will say whatever comes to mind. If we cry, he will cry with us. If we beat on his chest in anger over our helplessness, or describe all our fears . . . nothing bad will happen. He will still be there, still holding us, still listening.

Maybe he will ask a probing question. Or maybe he will tell us about a time he felt the same way. Then we can admit the crazy ways we have tried to numb our pain or fill our emptiness. When we weep over those ways, he will weep with us. And then we won't feel alone anymore, or ashamed of our feelings, or afraid of being exposed.

Because He, Jesus, has just taken our sorrow, and the shame and sin that once covered it, into Himself. We will be soothed by His compassionate arms and filled by the delighted love in His eyes.

೭ಎ

Recently, the nine-year-old daughter of friends whom we had known for years died after a five-year battle with leukemia. For the first few days, I struggled not only with grief over Catie's death and our friends' loss, but also with a lot of anger, which sprayed in several unhelpful directions. After ventilating some of this at my patient husband, I finally woke up.

"Lord, why am I so angry?"

It was His still, small voice that made me wonder whether my hostility was related to those angry feelings that had never been resolved during Brian's trials. Had grief over Catie triggered my silent pain surrounding those terrible days when death hovered over our home, too?

The next afternoon, when some quiet time opened up, I retreated to my bedroom. I asked the Lord to lead me into that cold, dark room of silent pain, back to the fear and anger. And as I recalled that gray morning when I had wanted to throw something at Jesus, I began to cry.

I sank to my knees and pounded on the bed.

"Lord, I was so angry!" I sobbed. "And I hated You! I hated You! I hated You!"

Then silence. A peaceful silence, as if the Lord had spoken and calmed a stormy sea. My bitter tears of anger became the soft tears of grief. I knew that I hadn't really hated the Lord with my whole heart, but speaking those words to Him released my honest pain. Even though I had beaten on His chest in fury, the Lord still folded His compassionate arms around me.

In time, my view of those awful days began to change. I gradually realized that if Jesus Christ had been visible in our living room that morning, He wouldn't have been sitting in the easy chair watching. That was my distorted view of Him as someone separated from my suffering. The real

Jesus would have been doing what I was doing and feeling what I was feeling. "In all their distress," the prophet wrote, "he too was distressed" (Isaiah 63:9).

I knew then that Jesus Christ—who lives in me—had taken my anger, grief, and fear inside Himself. He absorbed it on the cross. His passion was united with His promises.

My tears spent, I finished my prayer.

"Lord, I love You for feeling my pain and redeeming it all. I love You for not emotionally forsaking me. And I love You because Your compassion held me close even when I was angry and silent." The only thing that had delayed this healing moment was my poor perception of Christ's enormous compassion. (In chapter four I'll tell you more about why I know His compassion is real.)

Soon after that episode, my anger at people subsided. My sorrow over Catie became more centered around the family and less around me. My tears were softer and flowed more freely. And so did laughter. Ever since, there has been something lighter about my spirit. I know that my memory of that February morning seven years ago will never be the same.

The question I continued to ask was, *Why did it take seven years to find this comfort?* I remembered my own mother, and other friends, who had also struggled for years with these painful issues. Was there something I needed to learn about women's special needs in the process of dealing with grief and pain?

3

The Special Needs of Women in Pain

ॐ

My faith burns low, my hope burns low;
Only my heart's desire cries out in me
By the deep thunder of its want and woe,
Cries out to Thee.
CHRISTINA ROSETTI

I was halfway through my first cup of coffee when the headline on page 4 shouted at me: DEPRESSION STRIKES WOMEN MORE. I felt sorry, but not surprised. The surprise sprang from the subheading: "Twice as Much as Men."

The article discussed a 1990 study by the American Psychological Association which compared the incidence of depression in women and men. Ellen McGrath, a New York psychologist who chaired the study, said that one in every four women will suffer a serious clinical depression at some time in their lives, while only one in eight men will. "One of the astonishing findings is how often this gender difference is denied" in the health-care field, McGrath was quoted as saying.[1] She explained that the gender difference in depression has commonly been dismissed by saying that women are just more ready to complain, more able to talk about their feelings, and more comfortable using mental health services. But McGrath said the study shows that "this does not hold. There are true differences [in depression] between men and women."

The report also indicated that biology—e.g. premenstrual syndrome, pregnancy, menopause—is not as strong a factor as previously believed. "The major reason [for the difference]," McGrath said, "seems to be culturally implemented." The task force concluded that depression in women may be connected to our tendencies, as a group, toward passivity and dependency.

I see silent pain as the breeding ground or seedbed of depression. Our silent pain often lies dormant until stressful events provoke the symptoms of true depression. If that is true, learning to deal with silent pain—rather than being passive and controlled by cultural influences—becomes a kind of preventive medicine for emotional health.

PASSIVE DEPENDENCY AND THE PAIN PROCESS

The APA study indicates that women are more vulnerable to depression (and silent pain) because they have not been culturally conditioned to combat it. It suggests that their early influences and later desires to be feminine may have been confused with passivity or dependency.

Unfortunately, this is especially true of Christian women who, because of the fears and false messages we looked at in chapter two, may be uncertain about the difference between passivity and godly femininity.

How does this tendency toward passive dependence complicate the grief/pain process, or the resolution of negative feelings and silent pain?

The first problem it creates is a reluctance to handle our anger. It's ironic that even though men seem to be more emotionally repressed, they are also given more permission in our culture to express anger. Angry men are typically considered tough, not unmasculine. Angry women are viewed as harsh, strident, and unfeminine. Since unresolved anger is one of the main causes of depression, it makes sense that if women feel more compelled to suppress their anger, then they are also more vulnerable to depression.

All this leaves Christian women in double trouble. Down deep we fear that the anger itself is neither feminine nor spiritual, because of the false messages and shame. But when we bury the anger and then suffer silent pain or depression, we feel guilty for feeling what we feel. That's what causes us to doubt the validity of our silent pain. We can't accept either the sadness itself *or* the anger it covers.

The second problem is women's hesitation to recognize, respect, and receive grace for their individual needs in working through pain. Whether it's crisis pain or chronic, low-grade pain, we can become passive rather than responsible to manage our greater needs for relational support. Men, I believe, have the same kinds of needs when they hurt, but in different proportions and with different preferences for how they are met. Women in pain seem to have greater needs for conversation, for active listening, for openness and honesty—in short, for a mature, emotionally intimate relationship in which to work through painful realities. These needs—collectively, the need for intimate, emotional compassion—are the very things we sometimes find missing in relationships to men and, most importantly, to God.

That experiential lack of God's compassion is one big reason we get stuck in silent pain.

WHY ANGER IS SO DIFFICULT TO HANDLE

With increasing information about the stages of grief (or the grief/pain process), we have learned that anger is often a natural part of working through pain. But simply hearing this, even from other Christians, doesn't take away all our fear of *feeling* the anger that sometimes accompanies pain.

As we discussed in the previous chapter, one of the central problems for many women in silent pain is that *we don't believe important relationships can survive our anger.* Our need to own and process our anger takes a back seat to our greater felt need for security in relationships.

Thus, in a fleshly attempt to preserve our sense of being loved, we abandon a human responsibility—being a good steward of our anger. Dr. Mary Stewart Van Leeuwen, professor of interdisciplinary studies at Calvin College, identifies characteristic differences in the results of the Fall (Genesis 3) on women and men. At creation, God gave both Adam and Eve two central responsibilities: rulership (or dominion) and relationship (or sociability). But after the Fall, Van Leeuwen explains, men developed a tendency to let their responsible dominion become domination at the expense of relationships. Women developed the tendency "to use the preservation of relationships as an excuse not to exercise accountable dominion in the first place."

Van Leeuwen concludes that women tend to "avoid taking risks that might upset relationships."[2] One of the biggest risks many of us avoid is effectively using our anger, the very energy God has given us to respond to and grow through the pain of life.

The Little Girl and the Amazon
What do I mean by avoiding our anger? Most of us think we don't avoid it enough. Many of us will confess to angry explosions, and we have a hard time understanding why some say we need more anger. Who needs more?

Linda Schierse Leonard describes two general ways women tend to respond to pain and anger in their lives. Both ways are designed to protect us by avoiding the relational risk of expressing our anger. Some of us toughen ourselves and become more masculine in an attempt to survive, a pattern she calls the "Armored Amazon." Others tend to respond passively by remaining immature and unassertive, which she calls the "Eternal Girl" pattern.

Many of us have assumed both defenses in different stages of life, relationships, or roles. I have been both. In terms of my emotions, I took the Amazon approach by learning to suppress my feelings and appear strong. As an over-achiever, I could "handle anything" and often did so—at the expense of my own feminine self with its "gift of feeling." At other times, I was the Eternal Girl. I believed everything I was told by any authority and found security in going by the rules. As a people-pleaser, I loved to figure out what was expected and do it—at the expense of my individuality and humanity. This was my own way of creating security.

One problem with both of these immature attempts to handle conflict is our inability to handle anger. In neither pattern is anger transformed, as Leonard explains:

> [Eternal girl] women tend to be afraid of the fiery rage of self-assertion. So often they go to extremes to placate the other and adapt, hiding their rage under a pleasing persona. . . . But they then feel alienated from themselves and cheated in the end. . . . Rage can also be suppressed under an Amazon armor that appears seemingly strong on the outer level, creating a wall between oneself and others. But the positive power of the rage is lost because the armor is in the way. In both cases, the rage needs to be recognized and released before it can be transformed.[3]

Whether as Eternal Girls we suppress our anger, or as Armored Amazons use it to build walls, neither method effectively carries the constructive force of the energy which God intends.

Holding a Tiger by the Tail

When I first began to recognize that I had buried anger within myself, it was like having an emotional tiger by the tail. I could no longer ignore it, but neither did I want to face it and deal with it.

I soon realized, however, the relational consequences of not having "dominion" over it, not being a good steward of my own anger. During the worst times, whenever Lloyd and I would disagree, or if I felt he wasn't taking me seriously, I would overreact and find myself violently angry. I never screamed or hit him, but I sometimes felt like it. Or I became chronically critical.

"When the rage isn't consciously integrated," Leonard writes, "it often results in an unconscious attack on the partner, criticizing the other unmercifully and destroying all possibility for love."[4] At first all I wanted was to get rid of the angry feelings. (There are religious ways of "putting off" anger, by the way, that are nothing more than denial and suppression "with Bible verses on.")

It took some time before I realized there was something important in the anger itself. *Anger can sometimes provide the energy to respond wisely to physical, emotional, or spiritual abuse against ourselves or others.* Feeling mad is the inner signal to pour out our feelings to the Lord and then seek wise measures to deal directly with harmful behavior. Sometimes we can set boundaries or change our thinking so that we don't fall victim to abuse. Sometimes there are steps to take or the need for confrontation, and sometimes the energy may become prayer.

Even more important is another good use of anger: *feeling our anger can open the door to the very vulnerability we've been afraid to feel.* I realized that for me, the flip side of anger was grief. Something I wanted or needed very much had been blocked, and I felt angry at whatever or whoever appeared to stand in the way. Within that anger was deep sadness over something lost, something precious that was either gone or had never been attained.

If my anger can't defend me from pain or get me what I need by assertiveness, or if I choose not to use anger to manipulate others, then I am left with grief over my loss. I am brokenhearted and vulnerable. But within the pain is also the potential for tenderness.

Behind the rage are often tears. . . . Underneath the anger is vulnerability and the possibility for tenderness and intimacy. . . . So if a woman can learn to relate to her rage, this may open up her tender side and the possibility for an intimate relationship. Frequently when women express their anger with their lovers, they open up more sexually as well. So rage can allow a fuller love experience on both the physical and emotional levels.[5]

I remember how sad I was the day I realized that I had never *felt* loved enough by anyone to feel safe enough to be angry at them. There was always the fear (probably unfounded) that I would be rejected and abandoned, or that I would irreparably damage the other person or the relationship. Or the fear that if I showed anger, I was automatically sinning and therefore unacceptable.

The day I truly felt my anger and pounded on the bed was the day I fell more deeply in love with Jesus Christ, because I finally believed that His gracious love was stronger than my rage. I believed that He would never forsake me just because I spilled out my angry frustration and pain to Him. When I really believed that He would let me have my anger without reproach, He mercifully opened and filled another room in my heart.

I've discovered I'm not the only one who has spilled out anger to God and experienced His merciful response.

WHEN WE'RE ANGRY AT GOD

Yelling at God

C. S. Lewis suffered beside his beloved wife, Joy, in her losing battle with cancer. He described their experiences in his book *A Grief Observed*, in which he shares honestly about his doubt and anger.

What chokes every prayer and every hope is the memory of all the prayers H. and I offered and all the false hopes we had. Not hopes raised merely by our own wishful thinking; hopes encouraged, even forced upon us, by false diagnoses, by X-ray photographs, by strange remissions, by one temporary recovery that might have ranked as a miracle. Step by step we were "led up the garden path." Time after time, when He seemed most gracious He was really preparing the next torture.[6]

As he reflected on the agony of his wife's ordeal, this man of deep faith was angry and disillusioned with God. The next paragraph begins, "I wrote that last night. It was a yell rather than a thought."[7] In his pain, Lewis lived out his faith that God loves us enough to endure our yelling at Him.

Lewis' experience shows me that only as we empty out the honest truth rising from the depths of our souls can we make room for God's healing grace and truth to enter. David describes this kind of utter honesty as a sign of faith in God's compassion: "Trust in him at all times, O people; *pour out your hearts to him,* for God is our refuge" (Psalm 62:8; emphasis added).

Withdrawing from God
Another model for getting angry at God lies hidden in the story of a holiday parade, dramatically interrupted by a fatal accident.

It's the story of King David and his first attempt to bring the ark of God into Jerusalem after a long absence. David is well known as the "man after God's own heart" because of his poignant outpourings of faith and love, many of them recorded in the psalms. There is hardly a better model of emotional openness in all Scripture, male or female, than in the passionate language of this shepherd-king.

Our story picks up just as David, overcome with the thrill of bringing the ark of God back home, is dancing and singing with all his might:

When they came to the threshing floor of Nacon, Uzzah reached out and took hold of the ark of God, because the oxen stumbled. The LORD's anger burned against Uzzah because of his irreverent act; therefore God struck him down and he died there beside the ark of God.

Then David was angry because the LORD's wrath had broken out against Uzzah, and to this day that place is called Perez Uzzah.

David was afraid of the LORD that day and said, "How can the ark of the LORD ever come to me?" He was not willing to take the ark of the LORD to be with him in the City of David. Instead, he took it aside to the house of Obed-Edom the Gittite. (2 Samuel 6:6-10)

Whenever I had heard this passage taught, the focus was usually on justifying God's act against Uzzah. The Law of Moses clearly stated that no person was to touch the ark of God. But I had never looked closely at David's response or taken time to put myself in his shoes, and I missed a lesson in relationship.

Not only was Uzzah struck dead that day, King David was also shattered by an emotional lightning bolt. God's aggression against one of his faithful priests seemed grossly unfair to David, because Uzzah's reaction was more instinctive than deliberate, and an attempt to protect the ark. *How could God be so capricious?* David must have cried out in anger.

I sympathize with David's anger. After all, he had no warning. He was doing his very best to honor the Lord, certainly far better than his predecessor ever had. True, he hadn't obeyed the instructions perfectly, and he let the ark be put on a cart when it should have been carried with poles. But why such an extreme action? And at such a joyous time? (Much the same kind of questions we ask when tragedy strikes.)

In his anger, David may have torn his clothes or yelled

out his anger at the Lord without trying to hide it. He was mad and frightened. He had run head-on into the Almighty's inscrutable sovereignty. Probably still in shock, David abandoned the ark in the nearest field, an outward sign of his inward desire to distance himself from the Lord. Walking mournfully back to Jerusalem, David withdrew from God.

But the Lord did not withdraw from David. Nor did He rebuke David for his anger. He could have sent a prophet (just as he sent Nathan with the Bathsheba message) to confront the king about his attitude, but He didn't. The Lord seemed to be giving David a time-out period to vent his feelings without reprimand.

Neither did the Lord send a message of explanation to justify His actions and soothe David's feelings. In loving this man who reflected His own heart, God let David have his anger and fear without chastising *or* apologizing.

Recovering from Anger

During this time of withdrawal from the Lord, David carefully watched the ark resting near the house of Obed-Edom, which the Lord blessed. David saw that God, even in His anger, had never withdrawn from Israel. As Lord, He had expressed His sovereignty and holiness, but He hadn't abandoned His people. As Servant, He was blessing anyone who came near.

It was as if the Lord sat outside Jerusalem healing, bringing rain, multiplying the harvest—just waiting for David to come back out and receive Him again. After three months, when David saw how the Lord was blessing Obed-Edom's family, his heart opened. Renewing the ceremony and the procession of the ark into Jerusalem, David danced and sang with even more joy than before.

Rather than damaging their relationship, this open quarrel seemed, by God's grace, to deepen David's intimacy and his ability to respond passionately to the Lord he loved. The way David shed his kingly robes for a linen ephod during this second procession makes me wonder whether his sense of being accepted by God even in his anger had touched his heart and humbled his spirit. Those who study people say that we feel the height of our positive emotions only to the degree that we feel the depth of our negative ones. Because David felt his agony, he was free to feel his ecstasy.

David experienced the amazing grace of our Lord, who could obliterate us for our outbursts but instead waits silently in the shadow of the cross for us to realize how deeply He identifies with us—pain, anger, grief, fear, and all. When we grasp that truth, we'll want to shed our prideful coverings and open our hearts to Him.

THE TRANSFORMATION OF ANGER

If we acknowledge our anger, as David did, and we want to use the energy to build relationships rather than bury our feelings or blast others, how do we let the Lord tame this wild energy? I'm learning about three stages in the transformation of our anger.

The first stage starts when *we acknowledge and take responsibility for our honest emotions*. Spontaneous feelings are not sin but energy that can be used or abused. There was no lapse between the tragedy with Uzzah and David's admission of his anger. He acknowledged it immediately.

The second stage occurs when *we feel the pain by expressing our anger, sadness, or fear directly to the Lord, or to a trusted person*. This action requires a commitment of time to be alone with the Lord, or a person we can trust, to let it out. We know that the Lord knows our feelings even before we do. There's no point in hiding, and there's no need. Brief withdrawal may be a part of the shock stage, but being honest by pouring out our hearts to Him is a way of stepping out on faith that God's compassion in Christ accepts us as we are . . . right now.

We enter the third stage when *we let the Spirit of Christ within focus and direct this energy into constructive channels.*

This could range from confrontation with a person, to social action, to a change in our own attitude or behavior. Sometimes anger provides the energy to focus on the problem long enough to let the Lord change our thinking about the situation that provoked us.

After I had faced and felt my anger at the Lord over the traumatic times with Brian, my compassion for our friends who had lost their daughter deepened. I wanted even more to be emotionally available to them, because I wasn't distracted by my own anger at God. Now I could truly hear and empathize with theirs. More than anything I prayed for opportunities to reflect how much the Lord accepted them, with any and all of their feelings.

Another response I had after working through my anger was the desire to encourage emotional and spiritual freedom in others. Whenever I heard or read Christian teaching that prompted us to bury negative emotion in the name of faith, I felt angry. When I asked the Lord to focus that energy, He seemed to guide me toward writing and sharing about our freedom in His gracious compassion. I let my fears of inadequacy rest in my trust that as He willed, He would turn the water of my words into wine.

In other situations, my anger has acted like a warning light on the dashboard of my car. It tells me I need to let the Lord "look under the hood" for unresolved conflicts, wrong attitudes, or unhealthy patterns. I recommend an excellent book on this subject by Dr. Harriet Goldhor Lerner, *The Dance of Anger*.[8] Although she writes from outside a Christian perspective, her practical guidance is invaluable.

WOMEN AND MEN IN THE PROCESS OF PAIN

My husband and I have worked with support organizations for families with children who have disabilities. We've noticed how often mothers and fathers respond to the stress differently.

The mothers are more inclined to talk about how they *feel* about the trial and the challenges of caring for their children. Most of them welcome a program of open sharing, whether it brings laughter, tears, or angry frustration. Because of their own unique needs as women, they talk more about their child's emotions, relationships, and self-esteem. Of course, many women also get involved in the activities of such groups, but this is in addition to, and often serves the need for, conversation about their challenges.

The fathers would much rather *do* something with the kids or with the other dads than sit around and talk. Activity with others often creates what one friend calls a "silent camaraderie" that is comforting to many men. There are exceptions, of course, but rare is the man who enthusiastically welcomes a time to talk about his own or his child's pain. Typically, he would rather be active in fund-raising, information acquisition, activity planning, or the political aspect of disability issues.

Neither of these preferences is good or bad. They're just different. They reflect the healthy, basic differences most couples face. She wants to talk. He wants to do something about it. Both want the other to understand.

Until recent years, little had been written about the differences in the way men and women handle the grief/pain process (a term I use to mean the work needed to resolve any stress or loss, large or small). Most writing centers on the similarities of the sexes and their common needs as human beings for talking, seeking support, and achieving resolution. That's why I feel somewhat out on a limb even suggesting the idea that women have different needs than men — at least in priority and quantity — in working through negative emotions and silent pain.

One danger in identifying differences is that some fear that "different" means "inferior," and that it may result in wrong attitudes and actions toward women. Feminists' correct insistence that women are equal often leads them to emphasize how much we are the same as men. But as Dr.

Deborah Tannen warns in her recent book on how women and men differ in conversational style, "the risk of ignoring [gender] differences is greater than the danger of naming them. . . . Denying real differences can only compound the confusion."[9]

Perhaps the prevalence of depression among women, as indicated by the APA study, is linked to the effects of ignoring these gender differences. Tannen continues:

> Pretending that women and men are the same hurts women, because the ways they are treated are based on the norms for men. . . . Much as I understand . . . those who wish there were no differences between women and men . . . my research, others' research, and my own and others' experience tell me it simply isn't so.[10]

Some question this idea of inherent differences between women and men, asserting that men have the same deep needs to feel and express their negative feelings but are inhibited by cultural conditioning. This is the familiar story of the boy who is expected to be tough and not cry or talk about pain, so when he grows up, he can't and won't without compromising his masculinity. Environment certainly has its impact, but basic gender differences can't be denied unless we want to argue that God created Adam and Eve exactly alike.

This doesn't mean, of course, that men are emotional pygmies. I know men who suffer, cry, wrestle with anger at God, and cherish intimacy with Him. I have learned much from men who are emotionally adept and articulate. Many of them are gifted to bring a vital truth to believing men in this culture, to help them become less "macho" and more human, more Christlike, more connected with their wives.

But despite the exceptions as well as the common ground shared by both sexes, the generalizations about our different needs as men and women still hold true. Dr. Larry Crabb writes that men tend to feel greater needs for significance, and women have greater needs for security. Dr. Paul Tournier describes how men focus more on projects, and women more on people.

These differences shape our differing responses to resolving emotional pain. In my experience, women have greater needs than men in the following four areas: conversation, active listening, openness and honesty, and emotional identification and empathy.

Women's Need For Conversation

As I sat next to six-year-old Mark at our worship service last Sunday, I was glad he and Brian were with us for the church's celebration of Communion. Whenever the boys attend, Lloyd and I usually take the opportunity to whisper a few words while the elements are being passed. We share our thoughts or feelings about the significance of Jesus Christ's gift of life to us.

After we had each taken a piece of cracker from the silver tray, I leaned over and said some quiet words to Mark. He looked up at me hesitantly and said, "Mom, can I say this?"

"Sure, what do you want to say?"

Very matter-of-factly, he replied, "Girls talk too much."

Now I don't know what he would have said to his dad, but that was simply the moment Mark chose to let me know he had discovered a universal truth (with some modification). Not that girls talk too much, mind you. But that girls talk more. Specifically, more than boys.

I probably need no other authority, but I happen to have one. Dr. Willard F. Harley, Jr., Christian psychologist and author, compiled a list of the top five needs of men and women after helping thousands of couples improve their troubled marriages. Interestingly, not one of the top five needs is the same for both sexes. He identified conversation as the second most important need for women, although it appears nowhere on the list of men's most important needs:

Men do not seem to have as great a need for conversation with their wives as women do with their husbands. Women, on the other hand, seem to enjoy conversation for its own sake. Many women will spend hours with each other on the telephone, while men rarely call each other. . . . When men gather in conclaves, they tend to talk about practical matters. . . . But they tend *not* to talk about themselves or their feelings.[11]

One of the problems for women who suffer silent pain in intimate relationships with men is that it's hard to get their husbands (or significant men) to talk about their feelings or to listen carefully to the same degree that women need to talk about the issue or the pain.

If recognizing and talking about anger, grief, or fear is therapeutic, it is perhaps *more* therapeutic for women because of this gender difference. Paul Tournier writes,

Conversation that satisfies a woman's need must focus on the events of her day, people she may have encountered, and—most of all—how she feels about them. She wants verbal attention. . . . For a woman, real dialogue means talking about her feelings.[12]

Although men want to fulfill this need in women, Harley explains, they have a hard time, because men see conversation as a means to a practical end, not as an end in itself. Women also understand the practical importance of talking, but it's hard for us to explain the important emotional benefits in a way men will understand. Too often, we may feel that the need is not truly valid. Or that somehow, because we're not more like men, we're weaker for having a greater need for words, especially words about our feelings.

Then the false messages echo back through our minds. As we feel our differentness from men, we hear the inner accusations that all our talk about our emotions is not rational (doesn't make sense), not faithful (reflects anxiety), not loving (seems self-centered), and not efficient (doesn't accomplish anything).

So we stop admitting our feelings, or we admit them and don't talk enough to heal them, or we talk enough but feel "weaker" because we can't find validation for our feelings.

Result? Silent pain.

It's also important to add that the feminine tendency toward passivity (if we have it) can lead us into irresponsibility. There may be times when we're truly guilty of wanting to talk about our pain rather than doing something about it when it's time to act. That's when we need support from those who will gently nudge us toward responsible action or needed change.

But far too often, we place action *before* processing feelings in order of priority. When that happens, our actions don't solve anything, and may often make matters worse.

Women's Need for Active Listening

Women also have a deeper need for active listening than do men. If we have trouble finding those who will listen as much or as well as we would like, we doubt ourselves and the validity of our feelings. We may become silently passive, over-critical, morally impure, full of rage, or addicted to anything.

Christians may hear from male *and* female leaders that "spiritual" women shouldn't have anger, or don't need to talk about silent pain, or should just "do something about it." Or that the remedy for negative feelings is simply to start serving others and wait on God to change our hearts. Or, if husbands are emotionally or even physically abusive, wives should be submissive and pray. Or to overcome the effects of a troubled childhood, to forgive by way of a simple prayer, start doing nice things, and be confident that all will be well.

Christian counselor Dan Allender calls these "Don't-talk-about-the-pain" messages "emotional soporifics" — religious attempts to use God as a cosmic anesthetic rather than let Him be our true Healer.[13]

As women, we need someone who breaks the "Don't talk" rules, who wants to hear what we need to say, who can be an active listener. One who will listen with deep interest and empathize by mirroring or affirming our feelings, not interrupt with ideas of how to fix the problem. Someone who graciously receives us just as we are, who values our uniqueness, and who will ask caring questions to draw us out.

The ability to ask caring questions is an important part of active listening. As long as they're not threatening, questions show the other person that we understand enough to interact with her thoughts, or that we care enough to seek more information or clarify what was unclear. Questions can help the speaker to think about her own views or feelings in a different light or ponder other possibilities.

As I read Scripture I'm amazed at how often the Lord asks people questions. The one Person who has the most to say, the most wisdom to give, and the most solutions to our problems *asks questions!* In contrast, I'm often so interested in what *I* want to say that I bypass the blessing of simply asking questions.

Women's Need for Openness and Honesty

A woman not only needs more conversation and active listening, she also longs for the people she loves to talk about their lives and communicate their feelings honestly.

During a stormy season in our marriage a few years ago, I was feeling very distant from Lloyd and struggling with giving and receiving daily signs of affection. When he would say "I love you," I would mumble it back, and feel terrible inside. A hug or kiss almost physically hurt. I actually felt *more* distant when I touched him because the physical contact exposed the size of the emotional distance.

One day, as we were talking about serious problems and clinging to our commitment to work it out, I was finally able to speak the truth. "I don't love you right now," I said.

Even though it hurt, he graciously accepted my honest message. As often happens, truth begets truth.

"I don't love you right now, either," he replied.

This may sound funny, but I felt closer to him at that moment than I had in months. We actually laughed from our relief over finally speaking the truth. In the security of commitment, we could be honest. And we were more intimately connected in our non-loving honesty than in a pretense of love.

For the next few weeks, it felt as if a window had opened in a dark, stuffy room of my soul, and there was fresh air at last. If Lloyd put his arms around me, I felt more relaxed. And if we looked one another in the eye, one of us would smirk and say, "Remember, I don't love you."

I think that exchange was one of the first stepping-stones across the mire of those uncertain months in our relationship.

We want to be *talked to* honestly. I think when I finally stumbled on the question, "Lord, how do You feel about this?" I was expressing my need for openness and honesty. I wanted God to "open up" and talk to me about His feelings. Of course, He's been open with His people since Adam and Eve. The problem is with our hiding when He wants to talk, or with our closed ears when He wants most for us to listen.

The astonishing discovery awaiting us is that if we want to be found and want to hear, He is more than happy to open His heart.

Women's Need
for Emotional Identification and Empathy

No matter how much we want them to be perfectly available to us, parents, spouses, lovers, and friends will inevitably fail us sometimes. The often agonizing reality is that when we enter these vulnerable, wounded places in our souls, human failure can feel devastating. It can multiply silent pain. That's when we cry out for a perfect connection: *total emotional identification and empathy.*

This longing for emotional identification was portrayed in a TV show a few years ago that captured the hearts of thousands of viewers, most of them women. *Beauty and the Beast* transposed the famous fairy tale into present-day New York City, bringing together an assistant district attorney named Kathryn with Vincent, a half-man, half-lion beast who inhabited the New York City underground.

From lyrical exchanges on Kathryn's apartment balcony about such classic themes as courage and justice to physical conflict with violent offenders, the show explored the intuitive, soul-deep connection between this unlikely pair—limited in physical expression to earnest gazes and tender embraces. Their intense emotional bond was summed up in the irresistible message Vincent spoke to Kathryn in the very first episode, which would become the hallmark of their love: "Kathryn, there is a deep connection between us. I feel what you feel. Your pain is my pain."

Of course this prime-time fairy tale was just that: a fairy tale, far removed from reality. It could view life through rose-colored glasses, ignoring the gray shades of daily living. But this wildly unbelievable romance tapped into a deep cry in many women's hearts.

We can't make this cry go away just by being thankful for imperfect connections, important as that is. It is neither realistic nor necessary to deny our need for a perfect connection. The issue lies in how we search for it. If we expect to make this ultimate connection with a human being we will always be disappointed, even damaged. Trying for such total identification results in unhealthy dependence on those whom God never intended or equipped to be our final refuge.

If we are to find a perfect person who will let us have our anger and tears, who will listen to all our cries for help, a person who will feel what we feel and share a communion of hearts, someone who will never be distant, impatient, or indifferent when we are most needy, then we have only one place to go.

There is One who will talk with us as we walk through the garden of His compassion, who listens actively, who shares His own heart with abandon, and who carries our sorrows, weeps with us, and feels our pain as His pain. The perfect connection we long for is waiting for us in the deep, tender compassion of Jesus Christ. How we discover it and experience it is the subject of the next chapter.

PART TWO

HEALING

4

When God's Heart Breaks:
Discovering His Compassion

୨ఄ

The mystery of God's love is not that he
takes our pains away, but that he first
wants to share them with us.[1]
HENRI J. M. NOUWEN

The first time I heard about Rob Bryant was the weekend
I met his wife, Wanice, at a Christian women's conference where I was speaking. When she heard that our son was
disabled, Wanice came to me soon after the first session to
talk. We had something painful in common.

Rob, a strapping oil-field engineer, had fallen from an
oil rig two years before, which paralyzed him from the waist
down. As Wanice talked, I experienced the bittersweet bond
of similar suffering. In that sun-bathed, garden-like lobby of
our suburban hotel, we shared our stories . . . and our tears.

As we parted, Wanice told me Rob had written a book
that would soon be out. I got the title, and a few months later
I read the story with keener interest because of this personal
contact with Wanice. The courageous climax of *Lord, Lift Me
Up* is the three-day, twenty-four-mile walk Rob completed,
with leg braces and crutches, to raise money for the American Paralysis Association.

But tucked away in an earlier part of the story was another, quieter climax of courage that I will never forget. Just before he began the serious training for his Miracle Walk of July 1984, Rob was sitting in their living room tending second-degree burns on his feet, the result of a nurse's putting his insensitive limbs in steaming hot bath water.

Already feeling discouraged by this delay, Rob wasn't prepared when his four-year-old son Jason walked into the room and said to him, his eyes downcast and his voice barely audible, "I wish you could be like the dad in my book":

"What do you mean, Jason? What book?"

"*The Daddy Book!*"

"Go get it and show me, Jason," I replied curiously. He disappeared into his room and came back a few seconds later with *The Daddy Book*. I opened it and on the very first page it showed a dad carrying his son on his shoulders. On each page was a picture of a big strong daddy doing things with his son—like chasing and playing tag, climbing trees, riding a bike, and so on. As I looked at the pages and saw how badly Jason wanted me to be like the dad in the book, I couldn't stand it. But mostly what bothered me was the look I saw in his eye. It was disappointment.

"Jason, I'm sorry I can't be like this dad, but I try very hard to do everything with you that I can. I want to do all the things in this book, but I can't. I hope you understand that. It's not that I don't want to play with you this way, but it's just not possible. Do you understand?"

"Yes, I understand, Dad, but I still cry for you and me because you can't walk." That was what made me break. He jumped up in my arms and we both cried together. What happened between us was painful, but I was glad we had it out in the open. . . . I was proud that Jason had the courage to confront the situation and want to talk about it so openly with me. We both grew closer during those moments.[2]

With everyone else, I admire Rob's tenacious faith and courage to sweat, ache, bleed, and push himself beyond his limits to trudge down a hot freeway between Dallas and Fort Worth, Texas. But this tender scene between a father and son—an equally courageous walk through grief to intimacy—caused me to appreciate this man even more.

In the middle of his own loss and discouragement, Rob had the emotional stamina to feel and accept the pain of his son's grief and disappointment. He let Jason have his sorrow, and he cried with him. Rather than withdrawing because of hurt pride or fear of rejection, Rob could commend Jason for being so open and honest. What costly, fatherly compassion!

THE NEED FOR HONESTY

When I think about that story, I feel like saying with Jason, "Lord, I wish You could always be—in my experience—like the dad in my Book." And sometimes, like Jason, I cry, too.

Of course, the "injury" in this case is not in God, but in me. *My* senses are partially paralyzed. *My* eyes are partially blinded by wounds and sin and weakness. Therefore I feel and see only a portion of the comforting compassion, the shame-killing grace, and the deep, deep love of Jesus that can fill me "to the measure of all the fullness of God" (Ephesians 3:19).

So when the bottom dropped out for me five years ago, and I lay prone on the floor begging the Lord to restore me, I was admitting how paralyzed I was. With a handicapped son who needed constant care, and a healthy, active toddler, I was fighting through each day on an emotional string that was ready to snap. I felt overwhelmed. I felt abandoned emotionally. I felt forgotten by a God who promised relief sometime in the indefinite future. And I didn't believe I could go another step, even though I continued with inconsistent devotions, pleading prayer, and tearful worship.

I remember asking a friend over the phone one day, "What does Jesus mean when He says, 'Come unto me all you who are weary and heavy laden, and I will give you rest?' I come to Him and I don't find rest." And that's the same cry, though muffled or denied, of those of us in silent pain who never seem to find that deep inner rest that Jesus promises.

At that time, of course, I didn't know I still had unresolved grief and anger at the Lord for all that was happening, as well as pent-up anger at my husband, who was facing his own individual, prolonged grief over Brian's condition. (As I have read since then about parents of handicapped children, the spouse's inability to work through grief is the chief culprit in their 80 percent divorce rate. Strife and division are sinful actions and reactions, but they are magnified tenfold by repressed grief.) Those of us in silent pain probably also carry unresolved grief from the past.

Resolution of grief and acceptance by faith are possible, certainly, but Jesus says that neither can come until we face the pure sorrow and feel it. We can't be comforted until we have mourned. In the face of loss and our sinful reactions to it, honest grief is the death that precedes new life.

But I couldn't face the overwhelming grief that had risen to toxic levels inside my soul. One big reason was that I didn't intimately know the fullness of God's compassion.

People in silent pain are caught in a Catch-22. They can't feel their pain because they don't know or trust God's compassion, and they can't experience God's compassion because they won't feel their pain in His presence. My question, "Lord, how do You feel about this?" was my way of asking God to open my eyes and sensitize my heart to the beauty and emotional reality of His identification with our pain.

ENTERING THE GARDEN OF GOD'S COMPASSION

That crisis was the beginning of my search for the garden of God's compassion. I once thought that His compassion was a beautiful place I could visit, especially in times of crisis grief, but I felt I had to live in my semiarid section of town.

I grew up in West Texas, a truly semiarid part of the state, and my emotional life resembled the terrain: dry and flat. I remember my green-thumbed mother scratching out a flower bed for hearty geraniums and nursing a courageous crepe myrtle, but in Lubbock a true garden was about as rare as rain. Then I moved to East Texas. Trees, flowers, blooming shrubs, and wild flowers everywhere, any time of year! We don't just *have* gardens in East Texas, we *live* in one.

That's what I'm discovering about the garden of God's compassion. It's not just a place to visit in crisis, but a part of my everyday life in Jesus Christ that I deeply need to enjoy. In Christ, we don't just have the promise of God's compassion, we *live* in it.

I have to pray constantly, "Lord, give me eyes to see."

WHAT DOES COMPASSION LOOK LIKE?

Five years ago when Lloyd and I first sought counseling, I was asking the Lord to search me, know my heart, and change me. But I also asked Him to let me search and know His heart, especially His heart of compassion. I didn't have a sense of God as an emotional being. I needed to experience that intimate connection, but all I had was a "fax" of His personality.

I started by looking up the word "compassion." I found that it's formed by the Latin *com-*, meaning "with," and *pati-*, meaning "to bear or suffer." To have compassion, then, literally means to suffer or experience with another. Webster's describes it as "deep feeling and understanding of misery . . . spiritual consciousness of the personal tragedy of another and selfless tenderness directed toward it."[3]

Did I experience Jesus entering into all my sorrow and loss, my temptation, the "personal tragedy" of my sin, and then expressing selfless tenderness in the midst of my pain? I knew He was always present, always supervising, but my emotions pictured Him always sitting in that easy chair across the room.

Then I found that another word closely associated with compassion, sympathy, comes from the Greek *syn-* (with) and *pathos* (feeling). Compassion means "experiencing with," and sympathy means "feeling with" or "having common feelings." According to Webster's, sympathy is "an affinity, association or relationship between persons . . . wherein whatever affects one similarly affects the other."[4]

When I read in Hebrews 4:15 that Jesus can "sympathize with our weaknesses," the words leap off the page. They tell me that by His life in me, Jesus feels what I feel when I encounter my weaknesses. As I struggle to set my mind on things in heaven, He stoops to set His heart inside my agony on earth.

The weaknesses I struggle with are the limitations of being human—getting tired, hungry, and lonely—and the fallen tendencies of my flesh that lure me into sinful thoughts and actions. Because He was "made like his brothers in every way," Jesus knew what human limitations and temptations felt like (Hebrews 2:17-18).

But how can Jesus participate in the sorrow, anger, or frustration I have when I give in to my sinful flesh? What about the pain I bring on myself because of my besetting sin, or my repeated failure to change in key areas, or my compulsions that I keep in check—or fail to keep in check—by outward efforts rather than inner renewal? How does Jesus know how much it hurts to sin, to be less than perfect?

THE NATURE OF JESUS' COMPASSION

That question opened up for me a whole new appreciation of the cross of Jesus Christ. When Paul wrote, "God made him who had no sin to be sin for us, so that in him we might become the righteousness of God" (2 Corinthians 5:21), he charted the unfathomable depths of Christ's compassion.

The Cross and Shared Experience
When Jesus became sin for us on the cross, He experienced the *pain* of having sinned in every way that we have sinned. He entered into the desperation of depravity. Even though it was only for a period of time that Christ hung on the cross and lay in the tomb, I believe He entered a timeless realm of shared experience.

I think of those hours or days of Jesus' suffering God's judgment as a huge reservoir of His compassion. Because of what happened there, Jesus knows how I feel when I stumble. He knows what it feels like to fail, to get selfishly angry, to want something that is forbidden, to be enslaved to people-pleasing, to overeat, to give in to sexual temptation, and to feel the pain of *resisting* temptation.

The compassion of the cross means to me that Jesus Christ experiences and feels with us when we love codependently, persist in our compulsions, or overwork to feel good about ourselves. Living and present within me, He felt my angry explosions when I kicked the cabinet door, and He longed for me to find healing far more than I did.

Jesus' compassion does not mean that He is indifferent to my sin, or that He is frustrated and powerless to save me. He entered into my sin with me at Calvary in order *to identify with me and deliver me*. His compassions never fail, even when I am sinning. That is the continuing "good news" of the gospel. Even though I may not feel approval for my actions, I know that I am loved, and I will be rescued if I simply turn and cry for help.

My ultimate rescue, of course, has already happened. Jesus Christ has already been judged once for all, and I am already redeemed from hell and saved to become like Him. He has already delivered me from the domain of darkness into the Kingdom of light, but He isn't through until He enters the shadows of my shattered experience to pick me up and carry me into the light.

A Gut-Wrenching Pain

In the New Testament, the most often mentioned of Jesus' feelings is His compassion. Several Greek words are translated "compassion," but my concordance tells me that the word always used to describe Jesus' emotion is *splangchnizomai*.

I'm certainly not a Greek scholar. Vine's dictionary defines the word, "to be moved as to one's inwards (*splangchna*, or bowels), to yearn with compassion."[5] It's a visceral-sounding word that reflects a very visceral experience. Similarly, in the Old Testament one Hebrew word translated "compassion" thirty times comes from the Hebrew word for "womb," which suggests associations with the motherly heart.

In speaking of Jesus, the gospel writers reached for this unusual Greek word because it communicated something more than a passing feeling. Brennan Manning describes it well:

> English translations resort to active expressions like "he was moved with pity" or "his heart went out to them." But even these verbs do not capture the deep physical flavor of the Greek word for compassion. The compassion that Jesus felt was quite different from superficial and ephemeral emotions of pity or sympathy. His heart was torn, His gut wrenched, the most vulnerable part of His being laid bare.[6]

Henri Nouwen writes about the *splangchna*, "They are the place where our most intimate and intense emotions are located. . . . When the Gospels speak about Jesus' compassion as his being moved in the entrails, they are expressing something very deep and mysterious."[7]

Nine different times in the gospels—when Jesus saw the multitudes or an individual hungry, harassed and helpless, ill, or hung over from the effects of prodigality[8]—the gut-wrenching feelings of compassion stirred inside Him.

Then, without exception, He acted to relieve their pain. Compassion, like all emotion, is energy. It is the emotional energy for two distinct but vital functions: (1) to feel deeply another's pain, and (2) to take action to relieve it.

Between Compassion and Completion

Everyone agrees that Jesus' *actions* to relieve suffering showed His compassion. But His deep *feeling of painful identification* is just as important to me, because Christ isn't always healing, feeding, and delivering today in the same immediate way He did then.

For those of us who live in the time between Jesus' earthly acts of compassion and the final completion of His miracle, the consummation of the Kingdom of God, what does His compassion offer us?

For me, it is the assurance that *Christ's internal stirrings of compassion for me endure until He delivers me completely from the experience of pain.* He has already delivered us from the penalty of sin and ultimate death, but we still pray and wait for the victory to be played out in our lives, for His will to be done "on earth as it is in heaven."

Between the promise we believe and the fulfillment we look forward to—whether that fulfillment is feeling peace and joy, physical healing in this life, or the total bliss of heaven—Jesus Christ hasn't forsaken us emotionally. God's promise that His compassions never fail is the gospel of grace to our emotional pain. It means He will stay with us emotionally—without condemning—no matter what. Someone we love may be with us physically, but emotionally distant or absent. They may forsake us in our very presence by turning their backs emotionally. Perhaps this is how many of us see God, and, as the saying goes, "What you see is what you get."

But Jesus' taking on our sins at the cross means to me that He will never emotionally forsake me, even when I am a prodigal in the pigpen. The prodigal's father, before he ever hears his son's repentance, is so full of this inner stirring of compassion that he *runs* to embrace his child (Luke 15:20). God, my Father, even sent His Son with me on my "journey" to be with me in sin and moral death, and to bring me home again. Without His compassion, we would never "come to our senses" (Luke 15:17) and return to His fatherly arms of love and guidance.

Jesus' life and death reveal to us that *our God of compassion would rather be with us in pain than without us in paradise.*

This complex compassion has many faces. I have discovered two of them, like the two sides of a coin, that help me understand God's compassion in better balance: the tender side and the tough side of His emotional commitment to us.

THE TENDER SIDE OF GOD'S COMPASSION

God's Motherly Image
One of the most celebrated garden flowers is the rose. Tyler, Texas, a city famous for its roses, has a rolling, multi-acre rose garden that blooms each year with more varieties and colors than I ever knew existed.

God's garden of compassion in my heart also contains an exquisite rose: the blossoming of His gracious, tender, motherly role in my life. It's probably fair to say that the emotional expression of compassion is most often associated with the feminine strengths. And although He is our heavenly Father, the Lord also uses mother images to picture His compassion at crucial times in Scripture.

The reason, of course, that God uses such imagery is that He created both male and female in His image, and therefore He is reflected in the best of both. Because God calls Himself a "He" in Scripture, I will, too. But if Jesus

Christ lives in Christian mothers, then He must be Christ-as-a-mother in us toward our children. And if we as His children need the motherly touch of compassion, He is more than willing to give it.

There are books available now that speak to the mother-loss that some adults feel. Some even suggest ways to grow by "mothering ourselves," and much of the information can be helpful. I remember the first time I heard about these kinds of methods for healing, and it's not a pleasant memory.

During a counseling session a few years ago, I began to see my needs for "supplemental mothering" and the compulsions those unfilled needs were fueling in my life. My own mother, stressed emotionally and limited by having six children, a teaching job, and an alcoholic husband, couldn't provide some of the healthy nurturing she would like to have given. (And that she probably would like to have received from her own family.)

One of the few scenes that I recall from my preschool days was going into her closet whenever she was gone. I would touch her clothes, smell her familiar scent, and try to feel closer to her in her absence. That day in counseling, I started feeling the loneliness of those painful times, and I wept uncontrollably.

After letting me cry a while, the counselor gently told me that I would have to learn to mother myself. I'll never forget the feeling of utter despair that came over me then. It was even stronger than my original grief.

"How on earth," I wailed, "am I going to mother myself when I feel so poverty-stricken inside my own heart?"

The counselor began suggesting a few of these methods, but I was deaf to the prescriptions. Finding healing in them sounded about as promising as walking a tightrope blind-folded over Niagara Falls. I felt hopelessly childish and all alone in this drastic emotional immaturity, because I had never heard any other Christian woman speak of such a lack in her life.

Channels of God's Tender Compassion

There was no blinding revelation that suddenly rescued me from my grief—a silent pain that I thought others would find hard to sympathize with because it seemed so nebulous. I had many things to be thankful for, why dwell on this?

But I couldn't shake it. I could only admit my weakness and silent pain to the Lord, because I couldn't pretend it wasn't there any longer. Over the succeeding two years, almost imperceptibly, the Lord began to fill out the definition of compassion I had come to believe. And He did it through three channels.

His Word.
His Spirit.
His people.

Comforting compassion through His Word. One of the first ways the Lord started opening my eyes was by letting me see how He speaks of Himself in Scripture with tender, motherly images.

In Isaiah 49 Israel is about to be exiled to Babylon as discipline for four hundred years of idolatry. Nevertheless, the Lord reminds them that He will have compassion on them even there. Like the father of the prodigal, the Lord waits on high to have compassion on His people, even when they're sinning. But during the time of waiting, the Israelites were not so sure about God:

> Zion said, "The LORD has forsaken me,
>   the LORD has forgotten me."
>
> "Can a mother forget the baby at her breast
>   and have no compassion on the child she
>   has borne?
> Though she may forget,
>   I [the Lord] will not forget you!" (Isaiah 49:14-16)

This mother imagery surprises me, not only with its tenderness but also with its timing. The Lord is speaking this way at a time when His people's hearts are hardened and callous. But He realizes that under the oppression of exile they will finally feel humbled, childlike, and forsaken. They will reexperience their total dependence and cry like an infant who is alone and senses that her mother will never come back. Like a mother with her crying baby, the Lord longs for Israel to understand how safe she is in His care.

For the first four weeks of Brian's life in the hospital, something especially hard to bear was not being able to hold him. Because of leaking spinal fluid from the incision in his back, he had to lie on his stomach with his feet higher than his head. My instincts and everything I had read told me how vital cuddling was to his well-being, but I couldn't. I could stroke his skin, but I couldn't hold him in my arms.

In my desperation to find ways to communicate love to Brian, I played tapes or sang music and talked to him a lot. But I felt frustrated because I couldn't reach him with hugs or with words he could understand. I even prayed, however irrational it may seem, that angels would minister physical affection to him that I couldn't. I was groping for every way I knew, and some I dreamed up, to communicate the love I wanted my child to feel. I believe my efforts were a dim reflection of God's image in my motherly heart.

I recall those motherly passions whenever I think back to five years ago when *I* felt flat on *my* face, handicapped by sin, nearly suffocating in my own dysfunctional behavior, and out of touch with God's love. All of us are as helpless in the flesh to rescue ourselves from painful patterns as Brian was to heal himself. Like him, I felt cut off from the affection I desperately needed.

Yet because of His compassion, the Lord hadn't forsaken me. He was right there, seeking ways to let me know how forgiven, how safe, how loved I really was. When I couldn't feel His arms around me, it wasn't because He had failed, but because I wouldn't believe that He *wanted* to hold me close.

We see that in the last chapter of the book of Isaiah,

the prophet returns to that gentle, nurturing image of the Lord's motherly compassion:

> For this is what the LORD says,
> "I will extend peace to her like a river,
>   and the wealth of nations like a flooding stream;
> you will nurse and be carried on her arm
>   and dandled on her knees.
> As a mother comforts her child,
>   so will I comfort you;
>   and you will be comforted over Jerusalem."
>   (Isaiah 66:12-13)

What greater reassurance could I have from His Word that the Lord has a tender, motherly heart of compassion, even when we are weak and wayward? But even though I believed what I read, I didn't immediately experience this kind of comforting presence for my silent pain.

Comforting compassion by His Spirit. A few months later, I ran across a contemporary Christian song based on Psalm 131. I had read the Psalm before, but now I went back and combed through it like a love letter:

> O LORD, my heart is not proud, or my eyes haughty;
> Nor do I involve myself in great matters,
> Or in things too difficult for me.
> Surely I have composed and quieted my soul;
> *Like a weaned child rests against his mother,*
> *My soul is like a weaned child [against] me.*
> O Israel, hope in the LORD
> From this time forth and forever.
>   (NASB; emphasis added)

As I read these words over and over one night, the Lord touched me with the reality that *David himself, the king of*

Israel, a man after God's own heart, had felt the childlike vulnerability and need that I now felt. Feeling humbled by the demands of his role as king, David took his tender soul into his arms, like a mother would let a three- or four-year-old child climb into her lap anytime, just because it felt safe. Then, he turned his dependence for the ability to comfort himself (and to comfort Israel) and put it in God's hands. "O Israel, hope in the Lord, from this time forth and forever." Whenever I read that last verse, I say to myself, "O Kathy, hope in the Lord one day at a time and forever."

David doesn't record the resolution of his feelings, or the result of his prayer in some great experience. He simply exposed his childlike heart to the Lord—and to any who may have the same vulnerable feelings. By writing this song to be performed in temple worship, David publicly modeled a tender compassion for that part of ourselves we so easily neglect.

That's the encouragement I'd needed: confidence that the Lord has within Himself a place for me to be childlike, weak, unsure, confused, imperfect—and that it's still okay. Those methods for mothering myself had seemed so inaccessible to me unless I could believe in God's tender, motherly compassion. Because if it wasn't real, then all the methods seemed like whistling in the dark.

One night when Lloyd was gone, I was miserable. That day I had acted childishly by pouting over (rather than discussing responsibly) Lloyd's long hours and his inattention to me. I had also yelled at the boys for simply moving at a child's pace rather than hurrying to fit my schedule. As I collapsed on the bed and wrapped my arms around a pillow, I listened to the song by Twila Paris from Psalm 131:

> All I see is that I don't see what's ahead of me;
> I'm afraid my life will never be
> All I hoped for in the end.
> All I know is that I don't know where the road
>   will go;

If I dream, then will I find it so?
Will tomorrow be my friend?

All my plans are falling through and I don't
    understand.
Yes, I know my life is in Your hand,
But won't You tell me once again?
Sing me a lullaby, sing me to sleep tonight.
Sing me a tender lullaby, 'cause all my heart can
    do is cry.
Help me compose my soul, quietly take control.
Sing me a lullaby and tell me I'm Your child.[9]

Encouraged by the music, I imagined the Lord holding me in His arms the way I had many times held my young sons. Even the rocking, soothing rhythm touched my soul. It was as if He silently wrapped His Spirit around me and said, "I know how you feel. It's okay. I will hold you as long as you want."

Sometimes, like David, many of us need a place to retreat and be restored. A place that is safe and soft. We need a perfect parent's arms. From such a secure place, that night I was comforted by God's compassion, but I was also more able to listen without fear or shame to the loving guidance the Lord wanted to give.

Comforting compassion through His people. A Christian woman and grandmother, who is now a good friend of mine, has been leading small groups of women through the Yokefellows spiritual growth study for the last ten years. Four years ago, I first met Frances Swann and joined six other women to participate in this nine-month process of getting together every week to discuss some of the emotional and spiritual struggles each of us was facing.

During the year, with a commitment to prayer and confidentiality, we talked about things we probably wouldn't have shared in any other setting. The group was a wonderful experience of God's compassion, as we found Him sharing in our trials and our emotional struggles through one another.

But Frances herself also made an indelible impression on me. Without teaching or "prescribing," her leadership and open sharing of her own life gave me the opportunity to know a mature Christian woman with a level of emotional awareness that I had never before encountered. But after that session ended, the group dissolved until last year, when we reassembled for "part two" of the ministry, called Spiritual Growth Group.

I looked forward to being with the group again. But what I hadn't anticipated was that, as the weeks wore on, I would find myself so impressed with the spiritual and emotional health in Frances. I began to feel powerfully drawn to this woman. It was almost disturbing.

One day I asked for some time with her to sit down in her cozy study upstairs where the group met, and try to sort through these hard-to-describe, unsettling feelings.

"I don't know why," I began hesitantly, "but I feel this strong pull toward you which makes me want to be with you a lot and open my heart in a deeper way." I wasn't afraid to be direct because Frances had been graciously accepting of our weaknesses without preaching or compromising.

"But at the same time. . . ." My eyes started filling and my throat tightened. ". . . I'm afraid to draw too close, because I'm afraid that if our spirits ever touch, I'll be overcome with sadness and I'll just want to put my head in your lap and cry."

I knew that sounded strange, but the words were out and I couldn't take them back.

Her whole person seemed to melt into a compassionate repose. Her face softened, her body relaxed, and her eyes sparkled with a loving acceptance, without a trace of condescension. I felt a childlike delight in my heart. This was the same woman who had gently but firmly confronted unhealthy attitudes in the group on rare occasions. The same woman who was so adept in social circles that she could chit-chat with the most superficial society.

Even though my words could have confused or frightened her, she seemed to feel no embarrassment. Not even tactful caution.

Her eyes were brimming with tears, and she smiled.

"Do you think it's because I remind you of your mother, since I am from her generation?"

I hadn't thought of it before, but there were similarities. Despite being distracted and sometimes overwhelmed by the pressures of life, my mother loved the Lord and people. The vital difference was Frances's self-acceptance and emotional acuity—things my mother lacked, by her own admission, and had far less opportunity to gain. Far less opportunity than I have been given, and yet my own emotional "legs" are still weak and wobbly.

Frances's reminder of my mother gave me the courage to admit what I had felt but been afraid to speak.

"That may be true," I answered. "The reason I knew I would cry is that my childlike heart wanted to ask you the impossible. I wanted to ask you to 'mother me.' But I was afraid it could never be."

Then I put my head in her lap, and I cried.

છ

From the perspective of a year later, I see that I was reexperiencing the pain of my original loss of emotional mothering. Something no one, not even my husband, could understand. Although my mother had wanted to be what I needed, the Lord sovereignly allowed life's circumstances and her limitations to direct otherwise.

In the last few years, I have struggled through anger at God for allowing the pain, and am now regaining a healthy compassion for my mother's suffering. And mine. I have also gained respect for what she accomplished against enormous odds. With some help, my mother kept the family together, kept food on the table and gas in the furnace, and finally saw all six children earn college degrees. Like Rob

Bryant, she had completed her own "Miracle Walk." I have learned what I know of perseverance from her.

But that day in Frances's study, I was facing and deeply feeling the loss of emotional parenting in my life. Like Jason, I was now able to cry because my parents couldn't "walk" —couldn't be like the parents in "my book," the idealized needs of a child's heart. And as I talk more openly with my mother now, I sense how much *she* wanted to "walk," too. But in her weakness, she did the only thing she knew.

My mother has told me how she prayed every Sunday during communion, "Lord, hold these children by the hand and let them walk close to You." And I remember her sitting on the pew, eyes closed, unmoved by the wiggles and whispers all around her.

Thirty years later, I see how God has answered her. Through people—Dorinda, Barbara, Charlie, Lloyd, Frances, and others—I have felt His hand in mine and heard His voice whisper, "Rise up and walk."

That day with my friend was a special gift, because it was a face-to-face encounter with compassion. I went back to see Frances over the next few months, until the grief began to subside. She listened sympathetically, shared my tears, and helped me see that my parents' suffering was not only a source of sorrow, but also an investment in who I am and what I am becoming. Rather than take my heart to herself, she wanted to see it restored and whole.

One caution in this context: It has been tempting to let Frances become the focus of my idealizing devotion, but the Lord corrects me when I fall into that and helps me to see her "feet of clay." As one friend put it, such experiences should be like icing on the cake, never the substance of our personal value or our experience with God.

Evelyn Bassoff calls this kind of kinship with special people "reparative relationships," and emphasizes their temporary nature.[10] In these relationships, rather than becoming dependent on His image in another, we grow until we can take their compassionate expressions — their tender eyes and heartfelt understanding — and put them on the face of God. By His power, we see them recreated in our own face, to shine out to others in need.

That's what it often looks like when the Lord reflects His compassion through His people. I can say I have seen it — not perfectly, but more clearly. When I'm tempted to forget or to quit believing, I have the Scriptures, the Comforter (His Spirit within), and memories of God's people to remind me.

THE TOUGH SIDE OF GOD'S COMPASSION

The Face of God's Anger

Compassion has another face, too. In C. S. Lewis's *The Lion, the Witch, and the Wardrobe*, Lucy finds out that Aslan (the leonine Christ figure) is not always *safe*, but he is *good*. His feelings run the gamut of emotion, yet always within the bounds of love for his own in Narnia.

Even though the Lord is tender and compassionate, He isn't a safe, indulgent grandmother in the sky who simply pats our hand consolingly. God's compassion, I began to see, contains the full spectrum of His emotional nature.

When I searched for a deeper knowledge of the Lord's tenderness, He gently opened my heart to His tough side as well: His *anger*. Anger is like the thorn on the rose of compassion. It makes us careful not to abuse God's tender, emotional side. Such beauty is well protected.

But whenever I thought of God's anger, I usually had one of two reactions. One was to accept the truth, but then minimize it. In this response I was clipping the thorns off the rose. I would speak of God's outbursts in the Old Testament and of Jesus slashing His whip at the moneychangers without realizing what I was saying: the Creator of the universe *chose* to feel the pain of anger over us!

My second reaction was simply to deny God's anger by avoiding it in Scripture or dismissing it as irrelevant to grace—because I was afraid of it.

But if I really wanted to know the Lord's heart, I couldn't single out His "good" feelings as if I were selecting items off a supermarket shelf.

Held in the safety of His love, I was led unexpectedly into a renewed appreciation of His anger. I had, after all, asked Him how He felt about things. But I was still afraid.

I felt this same ambivalence as my emotional relationship with Lloyd grew. After a year or more of encouraging him to express his true feelings, one night I received a rare look at his anger, which he communicated with control. When I didn't handle it well, he made the painful but accurate observation that I didn't really want to know *all* his feelings, just the positive ones. And he was right. I was afraid of his anger. I had a lot to learn about intimacy.

One thing I'm learning is that, like compassion, anger itself also has two sides: one tough, one tender.

The Tough Side of God's Anger

At the level of the mind, I knew from Scripture that because of God's righteousness, His anger is always just and fair. I knew God was slow to get angry and patient even with the rebellious (which I could affirm from my own life). I couldn't explain all His actions in the Old Testament, but I was relieved to find out I didn't have to explain God. He can do that without me. And most importantly, I knew that there is no condemnation, no shame, for those who trust in Christ Jesus (Romans 8:1).

But at the level of feelings, the process of looking at the face of God's anger isn't that easy—it's much harder, in fact. Especially for women who have grown up under authority figures who raged out of control. These women have even greater difficulty relating to the tough side of God's anger. We instinctively know that if we want a fully emotional and biblical God, we cannot separate His anger from Him. But we can't face it, either. For me, that was because I had never seen its tender side.

The Tender Side of God's Anger

Then a few years ago, the Lord gradually began to change my perception of His anger as I read through the Old Testament Prophets. I had always shied away from this part of Scripture before, because I didn't like to see God angry. Sure, I read it and even studied it, but I kept it all at arm's length.

But I was missing something vital: Behind all these angry warnings and faraway promises lay the broken, bleeding heart of a supremely emotional Father. He didn't cast His pearls of compassion before the callous hearts of His children without confronting them with the issues of sin they needed to face. But buried within His righteous judgments were the sparkling jewels of His vulnerability.

Only a Wall Between

In Ezekiel 16, the Lord tells the story of Israel as a newborn baby girl who had been abandoned in the desert. With a mother's love, He took her home to nurture and raise her. With a father's tender care, when she was grown He adorned her with beautiful things and gave her His heart. And finally, with the passionate devotion of a husband, He took her as His wife and loved her faithfully, only to watch her go after strangers and scorn His patient love.

But it wasn't until chapter 43 that the emotional reality broke my own heart.

The Lord is speaking:

> "The house of Israel will never again defile my holy name . . . by their prostitution and the lifeless idols of their kings at their high places. When they placed their threshold next to my threshold and their doorposts beside my doorposts, *with only a wall between me and them,* they defiled my holy name by their detestable practices. So I destroyed them in my anger."
> (43:7-8; emphasis added)

God felt defiled and shamed by the way His people treated Him. When they worshiped idols on the distant hills, that was one thing, He seemed to say. But when they brought their idols beside His own temple, worshiping and adoring those lifeless clumps of wood "with only a wall between," that was the last straw!

In emotional impact, it was as if a husband had confronted his wife openly and repeatedly about her years of playing around on him, but he still decided to stay with her, hoping to woo her back to faithfulness. Then one night, in the early morning hours, she sneaks into the house with her lover. Thinking her husband asleep, she leads the man into the bedroom next to her husband's and hers. And there she betrays him again, "with only a wall between."

Can you imagine the agony? Anyone who has been rejected by a loved one, or left behind when another was chosen, can feel it all over again. Yet the Lord's pain and anger are deeper still, because He loved perfectly. And He didn't indulge in self-protection. He humbled Himself in love to become personally vulnerable to pain. He *chose* to feel the betrayal, anguish, and rage, and He *talked* about it. Then (wonder of wonders!), He directed its energy toward bringing His unfaithful ones back to Himself. That was the whole purpose of Israel's exile and her return seventy years later. Not rejection, but restoration.

That deep desire to restore comes from God's compassionate, parental heart. In Hosea, God tenderly recalls His nurturing care: "It was I who taught Ephraim to walk, taking them by the arms . . . I led them with cords of human kindness, with ties of love . . . and bent down to feed them" (11:3-4). Then, when He thinks of destroying them forever, He can't bring Himself to do it. Listen to the cry of His heart:

"How can I give you up, Ephraim? How can I let you go? How can I forsake you . . . ? My heart cries out within me; how I long to help you!

"No, I will not punish you as much as my fierce

anger tells me to. . . . For I am God and not man; I am
the Holy One living among you, and I did not come
to destroy." (Hosea 11:8-9, TLB; emphasis added)

God's heart was breaking before my eyes! Finally, I saw
the tender side of God's anger. At an emotional level, He was
"torn in two" by the powerful feelings that pulled Him in
opposite directions. God's broken heart was crying out, and
His compassion was changing His mind about His beloved's
future.

Letting Us Hurt Him
Why would the God of the universe, who could rightfully snuff
out the source of His anguish with a shout, stoop for centuries
to endure the pain of anger over betrayal? What kind of creatures are we that the Almighty would bear such pain?

Far from showing callousness toward Israel, the Lord's
anger exposes His free choice to suffer emotionally over us
and count it as the cost of relationship. *The God who created
all things is letting us hurt Him rather than letting us go.*

Like His Father, Jesus never bailed out emotionally.

In fact, it seems to me that Jesus sought emotional intimacy with everyone He met, even though it took different
forms. Intimacy is often simply a responsible, well-timed
openness about how we feel and think. By that definition,
Jesus was being intimate even with the scribes and Pharisees
when He argued and got angry with them. He was getting
uncomfortably intimate with their inner hearts.

"Woe to you!" He cried repeatedly during one tirade
against their devotion to traditions. Emotional intimacy and
honesty moved Him to connect with these men through conflict in order to ruffle their deadly complacency.

And it succeeded.

In stark contrast, Lloyd and I both have an inclination
to buy peace at any price. But after the first few years
of marriage and many circumstances that shattered the
peace, we started admitting that when we left important

issues unresolved, the result was not true peace, but a tense politeness. Underneath, a lot of hidden resentment fueled unloving behaviors.

In our dishonest self-protection, we were avoiding emotional intimacy and the pain and challenge it involved. On my part, I wasn't showing compassion toward Lloyd because I didn't dare discover how he really felt.

We struggle to remember that a painful, honest, but "clean" argument (one free of blaming or manipulation) is more loving than a polite smile and outward behaviors designed to hide our true thoughts and feelings. The first choice helps us know one another and challenges us to grow in love. The second only keeps us unknown and unchanged.

That's why, for me, even God's anger has become a mysterious expression of His tenderness. I recall Linda Schierse Leonard's description of how women's tough rage is so connected with their tender side of tears and grief, and how anger is tied to intimacy.

What irony! God's anger and His compassion fit together. They mean that He will share our anger at those who truly hurt others, or who hurt us. They mean that He has loved us sometimes through discipline, never willing to give up intimacy to avoid grief over us. They mean that He has stayed emotionally connected with us *despite everything!* He's not going to protect Himself by emotionally abandoning us, burying our pain and His—and with it the energy of His love, the power of His desire to complete what He began in us.

These two emotions, anger and compassion, ultimately collide in Jesus Christ at the cross of Calvary. Righteousness and sympathy—forever united—are stretched out and nailed to a tree.

੨ৡ

When we see the beauty of God's compassion, we face the challenge of simply believing that it's as unconditional and tender as it is.

But some of us still run into stubborn obstacles in our path to the garden of God's compassion. Like the man whose son was demon-possessed, we may exclaim to the Lord, "I do believe; help me overcome my unbelief!" (Mark 9:24). Perhaps these obstacles to believing God's compassion have been in the way for so many years that we don't even see them, or they're so huge that we could never remove them ourselves. Recognizing and getting through those obstacles is what we'll talk about in the next two chapters.

5

The Paradox of Sovereignty and Compassion

*The proud latch on to a few facts
as the whole, and rest in their possession.
But those who admire God close up
can't wrap Him up so easily; they see far
more than they can grasp.*[1]

STEVEN R. MOSLEY

I f God's compassion is abundantly available to those in silent pain, why do we have such a hard time believing and experiencing it? What are the obstacles on the pathway to God's garden of compassion that keep us from enjoying its beauty and comfort?

The answers to that question may differ for all of us. As I have struggled to embrace God's compassion, I've found a number of obstructions that the Lord is teaching me to avoid. The biggest one was the conflict I felt between God's sovereignty over the pain we encounter and His sympathy in the midst of it. Those two realities were difficult for me to put together. So, because God's sovereignty was most often emphasized to reassure me of my hope, I didn't allow Christ's compassion to be as full and rich as it could have been in my experience. I was afraid that wanting Him to weep with me in my pain somehow threatened the belief that He was working everything together for my good. To me the two seemed logically contradictory.

I knew the answer lay in the suffering of Jesus Christ, because He had experienced the worst agony any person has known, including being abandoned by God at Calvary. The hope He brought us by His resurrection has settled for all time the question of whether God can and will turn evil events into steppingstones to His Kingdom of joy and peace.

For me, the real challenge was to apply that assurance to my own struggle to discover the compassionate face of God's sovereignty. Could I really grieve the losses of life *in faith*, if I knew *for sure* that each one was allowed to accomplish His good purposes? That collision of faith and feeling is what drove me to ask, "Lord, how do You *feel* about this?"

CLOSING THE GAP
BETWEEN BELIEF AND EXPERIENCE

The testimony of Scripture convinces me that Jesus Christ feels my painful experience more than I do. His deep, gut-wrenching compassion drove Him to undo the damage caused by sin. *He came to destroy the very things we know He has "allowed" for the perfecting of our faith.*

"Though he brings grief," the weeping prophet wrote, "he will show compassion [suffer with], so great is his unfailing love" (Lamentations 3:32). For me, that verse exalts the tension between sovereignty and compassion to the level of a paradox. To our human logic it seems contradictory, but Scripture declares that *God grieves with us over the very grief He brings.*

I believe that in our sincere efforts to embrace the sovereignty of God and to secure the hope that it brings, we have understated the magnitude of Christ's compassion and what it means to our emotions in silent pain. In emphasizing our hope in God's power, we have denied ourselves some of the experiential comfort of His passionate compassion.

The Explosions of Life

When Brian was a year old and things were relatively calm, one of Lloyd's friends loaned him a book out of a sincere desire to comfort us.

The author began by describing the years of pain over his terminally ill son who died at age thirteen. Although a religious man, this father had trouble finding comfort in the creeds of his faith. We sympathized with him when he spoke of theologians who seemed more concerned with defending God's character than with soothing a parent's anguish over a dying child. "They had answers to all of their own questions," he wrote, "but no answer for mine."[2]

On a feeling level, having a disabled or chronically ill baby is like being a child at Christmas tearing opening the biggest present under the tree—but as the last string is untied, the contents explode with a blinding flash.

What was expected to bring supreme joy, appears to bring disaster instead. After the noise dies down and the dust settles, the world will never be the same again. And you grope in the smoky fog to find the card that bears the giver's name.

On the faith level, this is nothing less than a mystery. We knew God had fashioned Brian as a gift to us, and we knew He loved our son even more than we did. We knew He had watched His own Son suffer and die because of His love for us. We believed that His resurrection was a historical explosion that would eventually undo all the damage and restore the joy a hundredfold. And most important, we loved and wanted Brian with all our hearts.

Inside my own soul, I was clinging to those promises of God and my love for Brian, but I was still slipping inch by inch into the mire of sometimes oppressive, sometimes numbing emotional pain. Few were able to speak to that sorrow, and some enlarged it with comments that were as insensitive as they were sincere. So I became more and more hesitant to talk about the wound inside, because I wouldn't risk being hurt or "fixed" again.

When I read this borrowed book, it seemed to offer the sympathy I so desperately needed, but at a terrible price. The author decided to give up the ultimate sovereignty and power of God over evil in order to embrace His sympathy. To us, that was like giving up the heart of Jesus Christ's work on the cross and our hope in the resurrection—which we couldn't do. This hurting father's need was poignantly real to us, but his solution was no comfort after all.

If God Is in Control, Why Does It Hurt So Much?

"Explosion" experiences often send us into silent pain long after the original event. We find ourselves in the same smoky fog, even though the shattering event is long past. Perhaps no one heard it except us. Or no one else can see the damage it caused. Sometimes we've lived in the smoke so long that we don't even know it's unnatural.

That's why we seldom think about groping through the gray air to find the card that bears the giver's name. But the issues are the same. And giving up on God's sovereignty in order to embrace His compassion is no comfort for our silent pain.

Mary, whose father abandoned her family when she was a toddler, had been a Christian for years before emotional pain and irrational anxiety forced her to look at her past. It took years for the smoke to clear and for Mary to face her anger and fear over the fact that her heavenly Father took ultimate responsibility for choosing her earthly father and allowing him to leave her. When a Christian counselor challenged her with the goal of being able to choose her own father again—choose by faith in God's sovereign choice—Mary felt the "explosion" all over again.

"How can I choose a father who runs away and leaves a gaping hole in my life," she anguished, "and cripples even my ability to find the only God who can comfort me?" That's the agonizing cry of every daughter who has been abandoned or abused by a father and comes to the struggle of faith in God as the perfect Father.

If parents have the power to influence their children to trust in the Lord, they also have the power (even unintentionally) to weaken them in their struggle to trust God as a Father.

Sandra D. Wilson did a study comparing a group of evangelical adult children of alcoholics with a group of evangelical adults from nonalcoholic homes. She found wide statistical differences in their spiritual perceptions. By dividing spiritual issues into four categories, Dr. Wilson determined that the adult children of alcoholics were five to ten times more prone to have problems experiencing God's love and forgiveness, trusting God's will, believing biblical promises, and forgiving others. "This suggests," she comments, "that the very evangelicals who are dealing with more troublesome personality characteristics are the same evangelicals who are less able to appropriate the comfort offered by their faith."[3]

The heartache is that those who have the greatest need to experience God's compassion have the greatest struggle to believe it.

Wilson's findings don't excuse anyone from adult responsibility before the Lord, but they may give us more compassion for those who wrestle harder with God because of poor parental patterns. From my own experience, I realize this family influence doesn't mean that we're doomed, or that we're excused from accountability. *But it does mean that we have more homework than others.* We needn't feel like second-class Christians just because it takes more time, more support, or more grace to grow in these areas.

In fact, it takes more courage.

Causing Children to Stumble

I think Dr. Wilson's findings reflect some of what Jesus meant when He talked about causing children to stumble.

The passage comes right after the disciples were arguing about who would be the greatest. After calling a little child into their circle, the Lord Jesus said that if they wanted to be great they must become like this child. Then things got serious, when Jesus said,

> "Whoever receives one such child in My name receives Me; but whoever causes one of these little ones who believe in Me to stumble, it is better for him that a heavy millstone be hung around his neck, and that he be drowned in the depth of the sea." (Matthew 18:5-6, NASB)

I don't believe Jesus is talking about damnation here, but about the physical suffering of drowning. I think He means that a traumatic death would *feel* better to an abusive parent (emotionally or physically abusive) than facing the stark reality of what he or she had done in a child's spiritual life. Jesus isn't saying the parents are unsavable, unforgivable, or unlovable—but they are certainly accountable. "Woe to the world because of its stumbling blocks!" Jesus continued. "For it is inevitable that stumbling blocks come, but woe to that man through whom the stumbling block comes!" (Matthew 18:7).

Jesus' attitude in these warnings tells me that although God is *sovereign* over the selection of our parents, *He is not taking direct, moral responsibility for the pain and spiritual struggle they cause.* In fact, He apparently feels anger on their children's behalf.

During this conversation in Matthew 18:1-14, Jesus keeps pointing back to the child standing among them. After the difficult warnings, He again turns the disciples' eyes back to this child. "See that you do not despise one of these little ones" (18:10). After the story of looking for the lost sheep, Jesus says again, "Thus it is not the will of your Father in heaven that one of these little ones will perish" (18:14). The whole passage is framed by references to the value and vulnerability of children.

Jesus seems to emphasize how painful and offensive the effects of abuse and neglect truly are. Not painful or offensive beyond forgiveness, or healing, or restoration. But deeply painful for the children, and for Him! So painful that it drives us all to the grace and healing of God.

That is sovereignty and compassion in the trenches!

"Become Like Little Children"

If you're a parent, I want you to step out of your "parent shoes" for a moment. As you think again about this scene, try to put yourself in the sandals of the child who stands amid these imposing men. Just gradually change your point of view as you picture the scene.

You're watching and listening to Jesus . . . and feeling surprised that He's giving you so much attention. Every time He speaks of you (four times!), He reaches out and puts His arm around you and looks you in the eye with deep concern. You hear these big men being warned about how terrible it would be to hurt you, and how valuable you are, and how angels watch over you.

When you remember being unfairly hurt by adults, you feel that this strong, loving man would be angry about that. He would hold you in His arms and let you be mad and let you cry. You know He would never hurt you like that, and that He doesn't want anyone else to, either.

In this passage, Jesus Christ draws as clear a boundary between Himself and the personal cause of stumbling as anyone could. And yet Jesus is God, He is sovereign, the One in whom "all the fullness of the Deity lives in bodily form" (Colossians 2:9). It almost seems that His compassion overruns His sovereignty in these verses, because He centers on the suffering of the child and the responsibility of the adult.

Elsewhere in Scripture, of course, we find the balancing truths of God's power and intention to work His good purposes through any and all pain for His children, and His admonitions to forgive those who hurt us, because we have also been freely forgiven in Christ.

Becoming "like a little child" can help us see the

compassionate face of God's sovereignty. I never want to lose the mental picture of this story. This is my tender Savior, my heavenly Parent, showing me His feelings about whatever wounds me. When I will let myself feel the pain rather than burying it, I will feel like that little child again, vulnerable and precious to Him. I may not understand all the theology, but I'll feel safe with Him. And whenever I get hurt, He is the one I'll run to.

THE PARADOX OF SOVEREIGNTY AND COMPASSION

Even though we may not grasp all the theology, we still need to grapple with how we, as adult children of God, can embrace the mystery of His sovereignty and compassion. *We can't do without either one and still find complete comfort.* But we don't hear as much about compassion and sympathy in evangelical circles as we do about sovereignty.

As you may have guessed, the book I mentioned earlier is *When Bad Things Happen to Good People,* by Rabbi Harold S. Kushner. I think the tremendous popularity of Rabbi Kushner's book reveals the desperate need in our hearts for a fuller description and experience of God's compassion. And perhaps it also exposes a weakness in our Christian explanations of God's compassion. When we neglect a vital truth about God, the Lord sometimes brings our attention to it through the experiences of those outside the Christian faith.

Satan will attempt to grasp our weaknesses for his evil purpose. As the "angel of light," He will take a truth we have neglected and fold it into the sandwich of his lies. Then, when the world is attracted to God's morsel of truth, they have to swallow the sawdust-bread of lies along with it. The job of mature Christians is to "take captive every thought to the obedience of Christ" by rescuing the truth-morsel from Satan's deceptive table. We can do this by recognizing our failure and emphasizing anew what we may have understated about God's character. And once again, the enemy's attempt to harm the church will be used by God to help us rediscover something we desperately need.

The Mystery of Divine Will and Human Will

The debates over the paradox of God's sovereignty and humanity's responsibility point to the irreducible truth of both. That's why many theologians describe them as a paradox—two ideas that are seemingly contradictory, yet both are true.

God's Word attests to the Lord's sovereign control over the choices of all His creatures. Nothing happens that will thwart the final good plan for God's Kingdom. Nevertheless, He gives men and women a truly autonomous will. We make poor choices for which we cannot blame God. We make poor choices that either have been judged at the cross or will be judged in the future at God's throne.

God doesn't take direct, moral responsibility for our poor choices. But by His grace and power, He will work them together for our fulfillment within the mystery of His loving sovereignty (see Romans 8:28-29).

Thinking Christians throughout the generations have had to wrestle to accept this apparently contradictory, but perfectly scriptural, conclusion. I think the same thing is happening in the church today with the issue of compassion. *The coexistence of God's sovereignty with His deeply felt compassion is just as mysterious and paradoxical as the tension between God's will and human will.* I believe we need to enlarge our view of God's compassion until it seems logically contradictory to God's sovereignty. Not because it is contradictory, but because such a view reflects the truth of Scripture.

If God Is Sovereign . . .

One of Moses' conversations with God that has given me hope in the silent pain of Brian's (and my own) physical suffering is Exodus 4:11-12: "The LORD said to [Moses], 'Who has made man's mouth? Or who makes him dumb or deaf, or seeing or blind? Is it not I, the LORD? Now then go, and I, even I, will be with your mouth, and teach you what you are to say.'"

If the same Lord who died for me says that He is ultimately sovereign over such handicapping conditions as these, then I can trust Him to "even the score" in eternity. Whatever Brian or his Christian brothers and sisters who share in disability miss in this life will be made up to them in heaven. So much so, that God says whatever they have lost will seem like nothing—on that *future* day—in comparison to what they have gained when they see Him.[4]

But that's not all. In the meantime, God says to Moses, "I will be with your mouth and teach you what you are to say." The Lord knows Moses' weaknesses better than Moses does. He has already planned to make His strength evident through Moses' speech problems.

When Lloyd and I picked the boy's name for our first child, we had no idea that our infant would have spina bifida. The first night after he was born, as Brian struggled to survive, I recalled that the name Brian literally means "strong." Wondering if it were some kind of cruel joke, I cried out to God. He gently reminded me of His words to Paul, "My power is made perfect in weakness," and Paul's words to us, "For when I am weak, then I am strong" (2 Corinthians 12:9-10).

It seemed like an assurance to me that just as He had told Moses, "I will be with your mouth," He was telling Brian, Lloyd, and me, "I will be your strength." When I think about all that came out of the mouth of Moses, I am amazed: the challenges to Pharaoh . . . the words that echoed over the Red Sea . . . the Law of Moses given at Mount Sinai . . . and his most intimate prayer, "Show me your glory" (Exodus 33:18).

But I caution myself: *Beware of any expectations about what God's strength through your weakness will look like on this earth.* It may not be as glamorous as Moses' eloquence. However, by faith, I believe it will someday be revealed as having just as much power. For our life—our *true* life—is hidden with Christ in God. Those who appear to be last will one day be first.[5]

Moses had a speech handicap, so God became his mouth. Those of us in silent pain, who feel like we have a hidden handicap, struggle with a kind of emotional stammering that makes us doubt whether we will ever be all God wants us to be. But He has made us, and He sovereignly allows the pain in our lives. Just as Moses' stammering was transformed into a channel of God's grace, somehow, someday, we will be a delightful example of God's joy made perfect in us through our pain. I have no preconceived idea of what that will look like, only that it will come by His grace and tender compassion. And we will touch others in silent pain.

If God Is Compassion . . .

As powerfully as the Lord transforms our pain, He passionately feels it with us. In fact, He feels it even more deeply than we do. Who is more keenly aware of how far our experience has strayed from the perfect joy He desires? He feels more grief over all we have lost than we do, and He longs to restore us.

An episode from Jesus' life brings this longing into clear view (Matthew 20:29-34).

Near the city of Jericho, Jesus and the disciples were walking briskly as a crowd followed—full of curiosity, spiritual need, and perhaps silent pain. No one noticed when they passed two blind men on the road, because these handicapped beggars were there all the time. They blended into the Jericho landscape.

But Jesus didn't blend into these men's landscape. His footsteps and His name sounded like thunder to their heightened senses. When they heard that Jesus was going by, they shouted, "Lord, Son of David, have mercy on us!"

The crowd, reacting with irritation to these familiar beggars, told them to be quiet. Disability awareness hadn't reached Jericho, I guess.

But the crowd's attempt to shut them down didn't faze these men. They shouted all the louder. They had begged daily in the streets of Jericho. They understood grace very well, and they didn't want to let it pass them by.

The second time, Jesus heard the blind men, and stopped. He called to them, "What do you want me to do for you?"

If they could have, I think the blind men would have given each other a puzzled look.

"Why on earth is He asking us what we want?" I can hear them saying. "No one has ever asked us that before. They just give us what they want to give or what they discard. This Man doesn't look down on us. He seems to see us as whole people who know what they want and can ask for what they need. That feels pretty good."

That may all be my imagination, because they didn't hesitate a split second before answering Jesus. "Lord, we want our sight."

What was Jesus feeling during all this?

"Jesus had compassion on them."

That visceral sympathy somewhere deep inside Jesus stirred again when He saw and heard these blind beggars. I think it stirred Him not only because of their blindness, but also because of their silent pain. He saw the way they were rudely silenced, the way they had to claw their way through society's disaphobia (the fear of the different), the way they kept calling to Him with humble persistence despite the scorn. Jesus felt an emotional intimacy with those who were "despised and rejected by men" (Isaiah 53:3).

The paradox of compassion and sovereignty means that Jesus felt a deep yearning to deliver them from the very affliction He had sovereignly allowed. Jesus touched their eyes, and "immediately they received their sight."

People in silent pain can relate to the suffering of these handicapped men. Our disabilities may be hidden from public view, but they can cause the same emotional and social fallout that these men felt. Many well-meaning Christians want to silence those whose pain lasts "too long," just as the crowd tried to silence the blind beggars. Many people feel it can be an embarrassment to the faith if others don't get emotionally healed pretty quickly. But like these men, we need to call out even louder to Jesus, "Lord, have mercy on us!"

The blind men needed more than physical healing, too, and they soon realized that. After their eyes were opened, they weren't satisfied to go home. The very last thing we know that they did indicates that the sight they received opened their eyes to their deepest need. Matthew records it in the same breath with the physical healing: "They received their sight and followed him." Jesus' miracle changed them from the inside out.

People in silent pain need more than relief from their pain, too. Dr. Larry Crabb and others have pointed out that the goal of biblical counseling is not simply relief from emotional pain. Facing the pain and hearing what it may have to tell us are often the means to true repentance and change from within. There will always be a level of longing in our hearts for that perfect relationship and our perfect home in heaven.

But I believe there is a portion of silent pain that the Lord does desire to relieve, if we will trust the depth of His compassion in the midst of it. And when He relieves it, just as when He healed the blind men, we gain a greater desire than ever before to follow Him.

DOES GOD "USE US" FOR HIS GLORY?

I believe the paradox of God's sovereignty and His compassion speaks to a greater need among women for an emphasis on the person as well as the project. As Dr. Tournier points out (and as many witness), men in general are more productivity-minded, while women in general are more process-minded. Men tend to be more interested in *doing* things together, and in this shared activity they discover who they are. They are more willing to be a part of the bigger campaign, to be one player on the winning team, or to be incorporated effectively into a higher cause. They seek out common work or activities, which keep them related to each other.

Women, on the other hand, tend to be more interested in *being* together. We especially want to be valued and recognized for *who we are* as we serve. We tend to be more person-oriented and more sensitive to the need to appreciate others as people, not just as participants. We often use conversation to discover who we are and then find common activities to reflect our friendships.

Of course there are exceptions to these tendencies, but in general these gender differences hold true.

Men, perhaps because of their bent toward external productivity, are less likely to feel used by insensitive leaders if they have a heart for the final goal. But women, perhaps because of their bent toward the person and the process, need to feel they are valued as individuals, as much if not more than for their contribution to the work—no matter how noble the work may be.

Whenever I would hear the truth about God's power to arrange all our sufferings so that they would work together in a beautiful way for His glory, it did give me a measure of peace. But I was afraid to admit that it still felt like something was missing. When Jesus said the man born blind was born "so that the work of God might be displayed in his life" (John 9:3), I accepted His wisdom in making it so. But the idea of being "used for God's glory" sounded perilously close to the sad experience of many women who feel used for the glory of a man's work, or pleasure, or convenience, or blame-shifting, or addiction.

The New Testament passages about men's attitudes toward women all include the emphasis on valuing her, understanding her, giving up self for her, honoring her as a co-heir of the grace of life, and loving her. So there is no doubt that Scripture recognizes and honors the woman's value and her feminine sense of the person. Christ gave

Himself up for the Church, not in order to use us as deper-sonalized objects for His arbitrary ends, but that we might become His Bride.

However, an alarming number of women are used by fathers, husbands and lovers, employers, or church leaders, and as a result have difficulty relating to verses about God's using our suffering for His glory, even if there is some bless-ing for us down the road. That doesn't call into question God's good purposes and character, but it points out that women, perhaps more so than men, are frightened and dis-illusioned by the idea of being "used."

The Difference Between Using and Loving

When I looked up the English word *use* and its various forms in my Bible concordance, I found that the verb never describes God in His relationships to people. No word in the original language is translated "used" when referring to the Lord and people. I remember that old saying, "We need to love people and use things, not use people and love things." The Lord is our perfect example.

That doesn't mean that God doesn't involve us in His plan. We are to give our bodily members as "instruments of righteousness" (Romans 6:13), but *we* are never called instruments, because we're more than just our physical bodies. The only place "useful" is used to speak of believ-ers is in the context of the vessel image in 2 Timothy 2:21, and here the meaning focuses on the use of our physical bodies.

Throughout the New Testament, God's people are called "children," "sons and daughters," "friends," "the Bride of Christ," and "beloved." We are loved, blessed, empowered, filled, and purified. But never "used."

THE UNION OF GLORY AND INTIMACY

Whatever God's sovereignty means, it can never be asso-ciated with using or controlling people for a selfish or impersonal end. God's glory always appears to be something indescribably wonderful, which we in the Body of Christ will share with Him.

As He prayed in the Garden of Gethsemane, Jesus said He has *already* given us a measure of His glory. "I have given them the glory that you gave me, that they may be one as we are one: I in them and you in me" (John 17:22-23). I am moved to hear Jesus talk about glory in terms of intimate relationship. Being united with Him and with one another, we mysteriously experience something of the glory to come.

God's glory, I'm convinced, is about empowering us by filling us so full that we burst with a joyful oneness that wants to call everyone into the love of the perfect Lover:

> I pray that out of his glorious riches he may strengthen you with power through his Spirit in your inner being, so that Christ may dwell in your hearts by faith. And I pray that you, being rooted and established in love, may have power, together with all the saints, to grasp how wide and long and high and deep is the love of Christ, and to know this love that surpasses knowledge—that you may be filled to the measure of all the fullness of God. (Ephesians 3:16-19)

Far from wanting to use us as a means to an end, the Lord wants to fill us with a soul-deep confidence in being so totally loved that we are freed from ourselves to love others the same way.

On a practical level, I've tried to stop saying things like "Lord, use this person . . ." or "God will use you. . . ." I know I can communicate a similar idea, but as I let my mind be washed with scriptural truths, I will stop choosing those words. My prayer may sound more like, "Lord, let this person be so filled with the depth of Your love that her life draws others to love and trust You." Or, "The Lord will give you His love and boldness to. . . ."

Some women's hearts are in need of such a careful, biblical choice of words.

During Brian's early years, we found the most comforting passage on God's sovereignty in 2 Corinthians 4:16-18. We would read it slowly and repeatedly:

> Therefore we do not lose heart. Though outwardly we are wasting away, yet inwardly we are being renewed day by day. For our light and momentary troubles are achieving for us an eternal glory that far outweighs them all. So we fix our eyes not on what is seen, but on what is unseen. For what is seen is temporary, but what is unseen is eternal.

When we're going through difficult experiences, they don't seem momentary and light. But the comfort in these verses is that in eternity, if not before, the pain will seem light and momentary in contrast to what God accomplishes through it—the fantastic blessings we will be permitted to see and receive. But our circumstances won't *feel* that way until we have the future glory with which to compare it.

In the meantime, in all our afflictions (which includes our silent pain), God is afflicted (Isaiah 63:9, NASB). Even when we suspect that our silent pain is somehow self-inflicted, the Lord is present in us, feeling the affliction with us. He knows that, ultimately, it is His kindness and compassion (not condemnation) that will lead us to repentance (Romans 2:4). In Christ there is no condemnation (Romans 8:1). In a fantastic exchange, all our pain becomes His, and all His joy becomes ours. When we're willing to have compassion on ourselves by faith in His tremendous compassion, then our faith will begin to make us well.

The paradox of sovereignty and compassion is that as surely as we sit at Jesus' right hand in victory, He will, in the words of the poet, "sit by us and moan."[6]

Even in silent pain.

"GOD INTENDED THIS FOR GOOD": BUT IT STILL HURTS

Another well-known verse that is quoted to reassure us of God's sovereign, loving purposes even in the conflict of a broken family life is from the story of Joseph in Genesis 50. When Joseph's brothers were afraid that Joseph might take some revenge for their mistreatment of him, Joseph spoke these oft-quoted words of faith: "Don't be afraid. Am I in the place of God? You intended to harm me, but God intended it for good to accomplish what is now being done, the saving of many lives" (Genesis 50:19-20).

This was no glib response on Joseph's part. It had taken him *years* of pain to get to the point where he could affirm this truth.

The compassion of Jesus Christ appears in bold relief in this story. Joseph's process of working through the silent pain that followed all that had happened to him was a long, tear-filled process. It bothers me when Genesis 50:20 is quoted outside the context of the months of confrontation and painful wrestling with grief that Joseph experienced.

Circumstances brought the brothers back together, but the reunion did not take place immediately. After the brothers first appeared in Egypt to secure food in the middle of the drought, Joseph sent them back twice to bring proof of their honesty. He put money and silver cups in their bags to see what they would do. He waited months as they went home and then came back. He hid his identity from them, because he didn't know if they had changed. And he desperately wanted to know.

In terms of the emotional toll on Joseph, most telling of all is that *he wept uncontrollably four different times* during the lengthy process of reconciliation with his family. Joseph would leave the room because he was overcome with grief, and finally with joy, over what he saw in his brothers.

To me, this weeping speaks of years of silent pain that

has been bottled up. Years of painful feelings that have never been openly felt and released. Years of trusting in the sovereignty of God but never knowing the compassion that could free him to have his feelings about everything that had happened.

I have sometimes heard this account used to defend the view that all we need to do is believe God's good intentions behind our painful family history, forgive, and move on. And forgiveness is certainly part of the job of healing the past. But Joseph's struggle went on for months. He spoke harshly to his brothers at first, testing them to know their hearts. He hid his identity until the end. And the question left unanswered by the story is, What if Joseph had found his brothers to be unrepentant? Would all this reconciliation have been the same? Might it have taken even longer?

I would guess that even if the brothers had failed, Joseph's compassion would have moved him to save his family from famine. But we won't ever know what would have happened to their relationships. We won't know how much harder Joseph might have cried or how angry he might have been, if his brothers had shown themselves to be the same deceptive, cruel tyrants over his younger brother Benjamin.

It's important to me to recognize that *Joseph didn't say "God intended this for good" until after the good had been accomplished.* Joseph said it after he saw his brothers' new hearts, after he knew his father and Benjamin were still alive and well cared for, and after he had risen to a position that would bring about all their prosperity.

Joseph's words are certainly our words of faith in what God will do someday. But let's not be too hard on those who can't bring themselves to say those very words during the "prison years" — when Joseph didn't say them either. Let's let them have at least as many tears as Joseph shed in the process. And let's not press them to say his words until the Lord has put them in their hearts.

THE PARABLE OF THE PARADOX

Walking with the Lord Jesus Christ is a journey filled with paradoxes. "As the heavens are higher than the earth, so are my ways higher than your ways and my thoughts than your thoughts" (Isaiah 55:9). Because the Lord is beyond our limited understanding, Scripture is full of paradoxes.

This shouldn't surprise us. In simply knowing Jesus Himself, we confess that a virgin gave birth to a baby, that the Creator of the universe needed someone to change His diaper, that the eternal Word of God became an infant who could not speak, that a man was also God, and that death brings real life. Why should we doubt that Jesus groans with us over the very things that bring Him glory?

There's an event in the gospels (John 11:1-46) that reads like a parable of the paradox of God's sovereignty and His deep compassion. It's not a parable in the sense of being fictional, because it certainly happened. But it is like a parable in the sense that it is an illustration of truth in story form. In this account, Jesus' words and actions bring together His breathtaking power and His equally enthralling compassion.

The place is Bethany. You're probably familiar with the characters. Lazarus, Mary, and Martha were close personal friends of Jesus. They had shown Him hospitality many times, listened to His teaching, believed in and lent support to His ministry, and were well known as His dear companions. And then one day, Lazarus became critically ill.

Mary and Martha sent immediately for Jesus. With grief and unstated expectation they wrote, "Lord, he whom you love is sick." They believed that Jesus would drop everything and come to their aid. After all, He had done it for perfect strangers.

But He didn't do it for them. John reassures us that Jesus loved His friends deeply, and yet He chose to delay two more days. Even though He knew Lazarus would be raised, Jesus had to endure the pain of letting His friends wait on

God's will without an explanation.

Then He returned to face them:

> When Martha heard that Jesus was coming, she
> went out to meet him, but Mary stayed at home.
> "Lord," Martha said to Jesus, "if you had been
> here, my brother would not have died. But I know
> that even now God will give you whatever you ask."
> (John 11:20-21)

After Martha's exchange with Jesus, Mary was summoned
to the Teacher's side:

> When Mary reached the place where Jesus was and
> saw him, she fell at his feet and said, "Lord, if you
> had been here, my brother would not have died."
> (11:32)

John takes the time to describe these two faithful women as
individuals, rather than lumping their experiences together.
But the one element common to them both is the sentence,
"Lord, if you had been here, my brother would not have
died." It makes me wonder if they had been talking about
this together, since they said it in separate conversations.

In their desperate desire to understand why the only
Friend they could count on had disappointed them, the sisters reduced His power to a window of opportunity, which
they believed Jesus had missed. *If You had acted sooner*, they
seemed to imply, *You could have spared us this.*

How we limit the Lord in our attempts to understand
Him!

The truth is, Jesus could have healed Lazarus from a
distance, just as He had healed the centurion's son. For that
matter, He could have raised him from the dead by long distance. Mary and Martha didn't know or had forgotten that
Jesus could do anything, anytime that was in His Father's
will.

But healing Lazarus was not in His Father's will. I

believe it was an emotional struggle for Jesus to delay, knowing the sorrow it would bring His friends. But He did it by faith and by setting His hope on the joy that would come later.

The differing responses of the two sisters show us two sides of dealing with grief and discovering the compassionate face of God's sovereignty.

Martha—The Struggle to Surrender Our Desires
Martha immediately followed her statement with the declaration, "But I know that even now God will give you whatever you ask." (See John 11:22-44.) Here was Martha's attempt to show her faith, hoping that it might influence Jesus' actions. And Jesus affirmed her belief in His miraculous power.

"Your brother will rise again." But He didn't say when. So she fished for more.

"I know he will rise again in the resurrection at the last day," she responded. *But You could do it now,* she implied.

I think Martha was finding it hard to let go. Maybe she was still in the bargaining stage of grief. She knew Jesus could raise Lazarus, and she wanted Him to do it that day. Only she couldn't come right out and ask Him. She thought if she had faith and dropped a hint, Jesus might do something. But He didn't take the bait. He didn't tell her everything yet. Jesus wanted her to trust in Him, not in His miracles.

"I am the resurrection and the life," Jesus answered her. "He who believes in me will live, even though he dies; and whoever lives and believes in me will never die. Do you believe this?"

It's as if Jesus was saying, "Martha, let's talk about *you,* not Lazarus. Are you going to trust Me *right now,* or are you waiting to see if I give you what you want first?"

That question hits home for me as I struggle with silent pain. Am I willing to trust Jesus right now, before the silent pain disappears, or am I holding something back until it does? He's proven His love already. He's promised the pain will disappear one day. In the meantime, will I turn my thirsty heart toward Him and Him alone?

Recently I was reading *Lion and Lamb*, by Brennan Manning, and came across something that startled me awake. He said there are three ways to commit suicide: "I can take my own life, or let myself die, or I can let myself live without hope."[7] When I felt under the power of silent pain, I was letting myself live without hope, even though I knew Jesus Christ. But living without hope is not living by faith. No matter what I said with my mouth, if I felt hopeless, or went through the motions awaiting heaven, then I wasn't really living.

Really living is *believing right now*. Jesus was asking Martha, *Do you believe that you can live with hope even though you lose Lazarus, even though there is pain, since I am your Life?* That's what surrender is about for me. Martha needed to surrender Lazarus. I needed to surrender the demand to have a perfect relationship here and now. (Because even my relationship with Jesus isn't perfect right now, since I'm not perfect.) Whatever miracle we're hinting for, do we have to have it before we will place our whole heart in His?

Martha must have said with a deep sigh, "Yes, Lord, I believe." Martha knew now that the conversation was about her, not Lazarus. Would she rise from the dead of her insistence on having life her way?

I think her answer means she did rise from the death of her own desires. Martha found the peace that comes in surrendering to God's sovereignty.

Mary—The Healing Power of Grief

Mary had a different response. She didn't rush out to see Jesus and try to get Him to do what she wanted. She sat waiting for Him.

I think Mary had let go of Lazarus. But she may have still been in the anger stage of grief. She wanted Jesus to come to her. She needed some kind of touch from Him before she could face Him.

And He reached out. After Martha returned, she told Mary, "The Teacher . . . is asking for you." How compassionate of the Lord to call for Mary rather than waiting for her to come to Him. When Mary heard that He was summoning her, she got up quickly and went to Him. And after making the same statement Martha had made, Mary couldn't say any more. She simply wept.

I think Mary's tears were the fruitful kind: tears of pure grief that washed away the angry hesitation that had kept her from running to Jesus before He called her. Her anger melted into tender vulnerability when she saw her dearest Friend and said what had been weighing on her heart.

Then we are told of Jesus' response to Mary's outpouring of grief:

> When Jesus saw her weeping, and the Jews who had come along with her also weeping, he was deeply moved in spirit and troubled. "Where have you laid him?" he asked.
> "Come and see, Lord," they replied.
> Jesus wept. (John 11:33-35)

When Martha had subtly challenged the Lord's timing, He gave answers and encouraged her to faith. But when He saw Mary simply weeping in pure sorrow, He wept with her. *Even in perfect faith and assurance of the coming glory of Lazarus' resurrection, Jesus felt His friends' sorrow so deeply that He wept with compassion.*

Living in the Past, Present, and Future
What makes this story a parable of the paradox between sovereignty and compassion is its parallel to our history with the Lord—His past promises, His present compassion, and His future fulfillment. In this sense, we live in three different time zones at the same time. This truth can help

us understand the paradox of how God is in compassionate control even when it hurts so much that we question whether He cares.

When Jesus speaks to Martha about being the resurrection and the life and about believing in Him for eternal life, Jesus is giving them (and us) His promises. The promise of His victory over death, sin, and silent pain. His pledge that sovereign love will transform Lazarus' death and their loss into something wonderful through Him.

Those promises correspond to the Word of God, which we hold in our hands and in our hearts as the anchor of our faith. The Scriptures enable us to look back on the cross and the resurrection of Jesus as the historical witness that all will be well. Without that assurance of His victory over death and sin, we would have no comfort. This is living in the Past Time Zone: the promises we look back on.

After Jesus returned to Bethany and talked to the sisters, He went to the tomb and called out Lazarus, who had been dead four days. In the parable of the paradox, Lazarus' resurrection is like the future day when we will be raised together with all believers to reign forever with Jesus Christ. When sorrow and tears and silent pain are forever wiped away, and we experience the unending joy and thrill of just being with Him. This miracle is a sign to us that we also live in a Future Time Zone of the fulfillment of our hopes.

But the parable shows us that in the Present Time Zone of our lingering grief and not-yet-fulfilled expectations, Jesus is with us. He sees us in our distress, weeping over the pain of our lives. He is moved in spirit, He calls us to Himself, and He weeps with us.

Once we work through our bargaining and anger stages, once we quit trying to *look* spiritual instead of *be* spiritual, once we get down to our pure sorrow, *He shares it with us.* If we challenge His timing, He'll teach us difficult lessons. But if we simply dissolve into grief, He will sit with us and mourn. He will, as Henri Nouwen said so well, answer our cry "from the depths of our brokenness for a hand that will touch us, an arm that can embrace us, lips that will kiss us . . . and a heart that is not afraid of our tears and tremblings. . . . To us a man has come who could truly say, 'I am with you.'"[8]

Just as with Mary and Martha, Jesus' promises are past. Much of His miracle of restoration is still to come. But in the meantime—the painful middle where we live out our lives in the twentieth century—Jesus weeps with all His heart.

THE TESTIMONY OF LOVE

There is a fitting postscript to this parable in one more detail the Holy Spirit includes. When the Jews saw Jesus weeping, they had two responses (John 11:36-37). I want to take the second one first.

"Could not he who opened the eyes of the blind man have kept this man from dying?" they wondered. These were the unfeeling thinkers. They were puzzling over why Jesus didn't heal His friend, since He had shown His power to heal the blind man. Some people—and I have been one of them—react to highly emotional situations by shifting gears out of their hearts and into their heads. I think that's what this group was doing. It's a great way to avoid your feelings.

The second group was a little closer to their emotions. They were amazed at how deeply Jesus wept over the death of His friend. In response to the obvious sincerity of the Lord's grief, they said to each other, "See how he loved him!"

This was an exclamation. Jesus' willingness to express His sorrow openly turned out to be a testimony of His love to those who watched.

Do we ever think about the possibility that our willingness to weep with those who weep may be a testimony to the world of our love for one another? Jesus' example and its effect makes me wonder about the attitude toward funerals prevalent among many evangelical Christians.

This attitude affirms that the funeral service should be a positive witness to the hope we have in Jesus Christ: the hope that keeps us from despair in the face of death. And that is certainly vital. But what often goes along with it is the assumption that open, uninhibited expressions of grief may compromise that testimony of hope. Faith in sovereignty, it seems, should tone down some of our grief over the loss.

The power of Jesus' example at this most famous of funerals tells me that *both testimonies are equally important.* We should weep with all our hearts, if that's what we feel. Rather than compromising our hope and our faith in God's sovereignty, this honest grief can be a testimony to the world of how much we love each other!

Expressing our grief can demonstrate that we love others enough to let our hearts break with theirs in the face of deep sorrow. We don't have to grieve in the same despairing way as nonbelievers "who have no hope" (1 Thessalonians 4:13). But we must grieve our loss. *The paradox of sovereignty and compassion means that pure sorrow doesn't deny our faith, and faith doesn't rule out our sorrow.*

Paul put it very simply: "Rejoice with those who rejoice, and weep with those who weep" (Romans 12:15, NASB).

≈

Understanding the paradox of sovereignty and compassion is one of the first obstacles to experiencing the present moment, comforting compassion that Jesus Christ truly offers us in silent pain or any emotional pain. We are blessed when we mourn because He will feel it with us; and because of that compassion, His power continues to transform everything for our welfare and His glory.

But what about those of us who *still* find it hard to bask in the warm safety of His love? What are some of the other obstacles to discovering our compassionate Father and receiving His love, which we so deeply need?

6

Barricades of the Needy Heart

ॐ

Our doubts are traitors
And make us lose the good
we oft might win
By fearing to attempt.
SHAKESPEARE, *MEASURE FOR MEASURE*

O nce we manage to get around the fear of compromising God's sovereignty, it's not long before other obstacles on the path to God's compassion loom in its place. I've run into or tripped over many of them myself.

I think most of our obstacles to God's sovereignty can be grouped in two general areas: problems that interfere with *believing* how compassionate God really is; and problems that block our *experience* of God's tender compassion.

OBSTACLES TO BELIEVING GOD'S COMPASSION

In my experience, most of us struggle with three primary obstacles to believing that God cares deeply for us in our pain: (1) *comparing our pain with others' pain* can block our vision of the path to the garden of compassion; (2) if we manage to see the way, *a false view of faith as stoic passivity* can snag our feet; and (3) we may be deceived into leaving the path because *we lack healthy models for emotional expression* among significant people in our lives.

"Don't You Bother God with That"
A friend of mine recently recalled a childhood saying she often heard from her mother whenever my friend suggested praying for something small. "Don't you bother God with that," her mother would say. And the girl quickly concluded that God was too busy with important things to listen to her "little" prayers.

As extreme as this may sound, the central message is not uncommon in Christian circles. At lunch recently with friends, I asked one woman about her chronic back pain, for which she had had surgery. She started to answer, but halfway through she stopped and said, "But I just think about those who have it so much worse, like the Joneses." And we all turned our attention to the recent tragedy afflicting the Jones family.

Now, it's certainly true that the Joneses' trial is heartbreaking, and that my friend need not dissolve into self-pity when asked about her back. But where do we get the notion that the existence of someone who is worse off makes our pain less important? Or less deserving of God's full attention and compassion? "Is someone suffering more than you? Then don't you bother God with that," we seem to say.

Yes, there *are* times to contemplate those who hurt more. Such as when we are caught in self-pity. Or when we think we're the only ones who are hurting. "No temptation has taken you that is not common to man," Paul wrote the Corinthians, and we are reminded of this when we meet others who suffer. The Lord even arranges those meetings at the right moment, I believe. He certainly did for me.

When Brian was twelve days old we began our second hospital stay to begin the major corrections of his birth defect. He would need a more complete closure of the opening in his back and probably a shunt for hydrocephalus. We checked into Children's Hospital in Dallas for what would be the beginning of an unexpectedly long six-week stay.

After a lengthy admittance procedure, we finally arrived on the sixth floor, where a kind nurse waited to take Brian. I was physically and emotionally exhausted, but relieved to be in a place where trained people would help me care for my son. I "crashed" for the night at my sister's house, and the next day things looked a little brighter.

It wasn't long before I started seeing the other patients on the sixth floor. That first morning a mother clad in shorts and T-shirt pulled her son in a red wagon down the hall in front of our room. I was glad there was a big window I could look through into the hall without being caught as I stared.

The boy's head was enormous and completely bald. A huge surgical scar began at one ear and reached over the top of his head to the other ear. Although it looked gruesome, the boy's mother and the nurses acted as if it weren't there. I'm sure they no longer let it stand between their eyes and his. One-year-old Paul, whom I later met, was born with a massive deformity of the skull. His mother told me it would take numerous operations to correct.

But it wasn't until that afternoon that I saw Jenny. Her mother, too, was pulling her through the halls in one of the now-familiar red wagons, an IV bottle hooked up to the attached stand. Jenny's skin was tallow, her face drawn. She had leukemia. I had never seen the disease rake across the face of a child, and I shuddered.

Did meeting these children—and many others like them—take any of my own pain away? Not really. Nor did it make my pain any less important to God, my tears any less likely to be stored in His bottle. My cries in the dark nights that followed were never drowned out by theirs in the ears of heaven. In that sense, we all have a direct channel to God.

But that experience of other families' suffering did prevent me from feeling alone in the darkness. As just one citizen in this city of pain, I was no longer the lone sufferer—as I was, for the moment, in my peer group. I could cry in my deep hurt over Brian's losses, in my anguish over our helplessness, and in my torment over having to resuscitate Brian again and again. But I could never feel I was the only one. Never again.

As I read the Scriptures, I can't find one instance in which God stacks up one person's pain against another's. He never minimizes one person's emotional distress just because someone else is in greater distress. When we come to Him with a tender heart in pain, no matter how large or small the problem, He gives us His full attention and His full compassion.

"Come to me, all you who are weary and burdened," Jesus said. Not you who are the *most* weary and burdened, but *all* who feel burdened. "In all their affliction, he was afflicted," Isaiah wrote. Not in the *worst* of their afflictions, but in *all* their afflictions. "Blessed are those who mourn, for they will be comforted," Jesus promised everyone. Not those who were *most* deeply hurt, but *anyone* who grieves in God's presence.

I know I'm only one of thousands of parents who have put a Band-Aid on a bump—not a cut or an abrasion, just a bump. Why? Because four-year-old Mark was concerned about it, and it hurt, and in his mind, what hurts needs a Band-Aid. But that flesh-colored piece of sticky material wasn't the only thing Mark needed. He needed a loving parent to acknowledge the pain and to understand its importance, because *he* is important. When Mark gets a bruise or a cut, he doesn't think about his big brother's wheelchair or numerous surgical scars. And I'm not going to remind him, either.

This obstacle to believing God's compassion—that He compares our pains and is compassionate with the big ones but not with the small—doesn't need to block our vision of the path to His comfort.

"Big Girls Don't Cry"
A second problem we face when we try to sort through silent pain is *a false view of faith as stoic passivity*. We can call this the

"Big girls don't cry" assumption. It's a form of stoicism, not Christian faith.

Stoicism goes back to ancient Greece and the belief that reason should dominate and control emotion. The Stoics considered *apatheia,* the basic lack of emotion, a primary attribute of God, who was venerated as pure reason.

This philosophical system influences our Christian beliefs today, especially in our attempts to suppress emotion. When pain comes, we tell ourselves, just trust the Lord and the pain will diminish. When disappointment comes, just think of future heavenly perfections and the anguish will subside. When life throttles you, turn the other emotional cheek.

No one shows me the imbalance of these false assumptions better than Jesus. "Blessed are those who mourn." How can we believe Him if we think grieving shows a lack of faith? "For they will be comforted." There is the beauty of His promise. *I cannot be comforted until I have felt my pain in His presence.*

When I feel pure sorrow—sadness due to any kind of loss, large or small—it doesn't mean I have lost faith. Jesus wept at the grave of Lazarus *even as He believed* in the coming glory of Lazarus' resurrection. He wept on other occasions, too, yet Scripture says He was without sin.

We need to sound two cautions here. First, the Lord doesn't want us to fall into self-pity, which the dictionary defines as "self-indulgent lingering on one's own sorrows or misfortunes."[1] Self-indulging our grief implies that we have drunk more than the cup of sorrow allotted to us. "Lingering" suggests that we have stayed too long in our sorrow, that the days of mourning are past.

However, the timing of the comfort process is a matter of individual conscience. We can't judge when another person in pain should change out of her sackcloth and throw away her ashes. We mustn't rush her for our own convenience, our own emotional comfort—or, worse yet, to reassure ourselves that God is still working. If we push the mourner into prematurely abandoning her sorrow so that she misses the comfort of God, she may retain a residue of bitterness, a silent pain.

The second caution is that in our pure sorrow we don't have to fall into despair. Despair is a loss of hope and confidence in God's loving power to transform our sufferings. King David often knew sorrow, but when his soul drifted into despair, he remembered God's faithfulness and encouraged himself. "Why are you in despair, O my soul? . . . Hope in God, for I shall again praise Him" (Psalm 42:5, NASB).

Tim Hansel says he has given his life to learning one verse of Scripture: "Because the Lord is my shepherd, I have everything I need!" (Psalm 23:1, TLB). In relation to sorrow and joy, this verse means that for him, joy is in believing that even during loss and grief, he still has everything that is vital for his welfare. That's God's promise.

Pure sorrow, I discover, has nothing to do with faith. Sorrow is the sadness I feel between the moment of my loss or pain and the moment I am reassured in my emotional being that I still have everything I need. During all this time I can, by grace, maintain faith that the Lord is providing for all my needs. *But my faith does not prevent my sorrow, and my sorrow does not deny my faith.* As the writer of Ecclesiastes tells us, "There is a time to weep . . . a time to mourn" (3:4).

When your feet get tangled in the snare of mistaking stoicism for strong faith, you will bury your pain and, with it, any hope of being fully comforted. Look to Jesus' example of bearing grief and let God's Word cut through this false view of faith. Trust Him to open the pathway—through your pain—to the garden of His compassion.

"My Dad Never Cried"

The third deception on the path to believing God's comfort is *inadequate modeling of emotional expression by significant people in our lives.* What happens when we as children grow up around adults who don't handle their feelings in healthy ways?

How are you to view tears as fully human if you never saw your dad cry? How are you to affirm the expression of sorrow in the healing process if all you saw was your mother burying her feelings, pouting silently, or running into her room with a slam of the door to cry into a pillow? Of course, the Lord Himself has given us the perfect model in Jesus Christ. But we need other models, too—"with skin on."

A month or two after my father's suicide, I drove to the home of my church's minister. Timidly I rang the doorbell, and his wife came to the door and asked me in. Reverend Wilcox wasn't there, but she would be glad to tell him I had come, she said. I sat awkwardly on the couch for a few minutes of small talk and then excused myself. I never went back.

I was searching. Searching for the pathway through grief. All I knew was that I was overwhelmed, and I sensed that I wasn't getting anywhere. Attending college classes and working part time, I was going on as if nothing had happened. But the minister's absence that night, and in the following days, symbolized an awful hole in my life. A hole where a model of grieving should have been. I needed a father to show me the way through grief, and mine was gone forever . . . precisely because he had never been shown the way himself.

I think of 2 Corinthians 1:3-4, when God puts His "skin on" in the form of the Body of Christ:

> Praise be to the God and Father of our Lord Jesus Christ, the Father of compassion and the God of all comfort, who comforts us in all our troubles, so that we can comfort those in any trouble with the comfort we ourselves have received from God.

That's our modeling. *We are to be models for one another because God, the Father of compassion, has begun the process Himself.* He has given us the example of His Son, and we are to carry out that example for a world in need.

And what is Jesus' model of receiving comfort?

As I read about His life, I see that He spent time alone with the Father. He poured out the deepest pains of his heart in all honesty. He described the hurtful things around Him. He sought the prayers and comfort of friends. And when they failed Him, He confronted them. He wept until He had wept enough. He cried out when He felt forsaken. And in the worst agony of His life, He committed His spirit to the Father of all comfort, even when He felt no comfort.

I wish I could describe an easier way, but I can't. The Model we are to follow took the hard road to compassion. When we model for others, we cannot and should not make it appear any other way, for that would be a lie. If we sugarcoat it, they will bite through it only to taste gall—and become disillusioned, and quit. They may blame God for not living up to their earthly model's rosy picture of Him. We have an obligation, just like Jesus did, to tell it like it is, and provide evidence with our lives that someone else has faced the pain and survived.

I think of the man who was asked to speak at the funeral of a teenager because he, too, had lost his teenage son. As he looked down on the front row at the grieving parents of this seventeen-year-old girl, he had one simple message.

"I know you would like for me to stand up here and tell you exactly how my wife and I endured the first year after our son's death, exactly how the Lord sustained us. But I can't. I cannot tell you how we got through," and he paused as he choked back tears. "But I can promise one thing. Jesus will show you the way. Jesus will show you the way."

It's my guess that this man came alongside these newly bereaved parents in the year that followed. I doubt he had many answers, but he had a sympathetic heart and a listening ear. He probably wept with them and told them about his own grief, and the many stages and feelings he and his wife encountered. They probably shared stories about their deceased children. Then they wept some more. And after they had wiped the tears, they could smile and embrace.

This friend could not tell them the way, but he could be a model of Christ Himself.

When you are deceived and lured to another path, away from God's compassion, because you haven't had a model to follow, get out the map of 2 Corinthians 1:3-4 and ask the Lord for help in finding the way through silent pain. Ask Him to show you another Christian who has taken the path. Pray for His guidance. Ask your friend to tell you her story of grief and comfort.

Let others be a channel of His compassion. If there are support groups that speak to your silent pain, consider them in prayer. Silence isolates. It is harder to be deceived when we have fellow-travelers, and that is what we can be for one another.

But remember that the models "with skin on" are earthly comforters. Look to the divine Model of comfort as your truest Guide for staying on the path. Search Scripture for His ways of finding grace to help in time of need, for He sympathizes with our weaknesses. He feels our sorrows. Let Him bear your silent pain with you.

OBSTACLES TO EXPERIENCING GOD'S COMPASSION

I think there are three major stumbling blocks to our experience of God as a tender comforting refuge. (1) *Repression,* or denial of emotion, heads the list for Christians in casting darkness over the path. (2) If we get through the darkness, a vague sense of *shame or worthlessness* may blow a stiff wind in our face. (3) The final roadblock—the only one God erects—is *known, unconfessed sin* in our lives. Even then, His compassion never fails to agonize in drawing us back to Himself.

Pain? What Pain?

Many of us learn very early that the fastest way to avoid the pain of a bad feeling is not to have it. Although we all have feelings, repression simply means that we don't feel or appropriately express them. We cover up. As children, we may see this modeled or, because of immaturity or fear, we may just try it. If it works to shield us from pain, we do it again. Then it becomes a habit. We may even be rewarded by approval from adults who tell us how mature we are.

Reasons behind emotional repression. Why do we engage in emotional repression? The reasons could fill volumes, but the first one I encountered was that *I assumed negative feelings themselves were bad.* In other words, I couldn't "be good" and have those feelings, because I thought the only way to express them was sinful.

But Christian counselor David Carlson argues that although burying our feelings may appear to avoid sin, it actually prevents deep, lasting change by covering the symptoms of the root problem and lowering self-esteem.[2]

Another reason we tend to deny our emotions, especially grief, is our *fear of being overwhelmed* by them. We discussed this in chapter two as a source of silent pain, but it pops up again as an obstacle to God's compassion in the present. Better to let sleeping dogs lie, we reason, because we don't know how they will act when awakened. Judith Viorst describes it well:

> We may . . . unconsciously fear that if once we started weeping, we'd never stop, or that we would have a breakdown or go insane, or that the weight of our grief would crush us or drive away those around us, or that all of our earlier losses would swamp us again.[3]

The helpful truth I learned about this fear is that the emotions we feel over *present* trials will rarely be overwhelming. They are feelings we have; they don't have us. But whenever we do feel overwhelmed by grief, fear, anger, or shame, it may be a sign that we are carrying past, unresolved emotions into the present.

That's why it was important for me to deal with the past in order to shed the fear of overwhelming feelings. Now that much has been dealt with, the "overwhelm factor" is gone. But the Lord had to run some of the "ghosts" of unresolved pain out of the dark rooms of my soul before I could live there in peace.

One of those "ghosts" was the memory of that dreary January morning when I sat with my mother and five brothers and sisters near the casket and open grave of my father. Two days earlier, the police had found a .45 caliber pistol and a note beside his body in the apartment where he had lived since the divorce.

As I squirmed on the cold metal chair, men lowered the casket into the ground, and the minister came up to each of us to offer comfort. Probably because I was almost tearless, he put his hand on my shoulder and quietly said, "You have been very strong."

At that moment and for years afterward, I believed him. I was deathly afraid of my anguish, and I believed that I was strong and couldn't be broken by feelings I refused to feel.

It wasn't a new practice. The same method I used that cold morning sitting on a hard chair, I had perfected on many warm nights lying in a soft bed. The nights Daddy didn't come home until long after we should have been asleep. I can still feel the oppressive dread that had no name.

On those nights, Daddy just wouldn't come home. That meant that by 6:15 p.m. we knew what to expect. We did homework. Went to bed. Said our prayers. No one ever asked where Dad was. No one ever cried or complained. Then, at two or three in the morning, I would awaken to the sound of his car driving in. Or I would hear him thud against the wall as he stumbled down the hall to our room.

Dad had to pass through our room to get to his. As he came by, I would pretend to be asleep. I could smell stale alcohol and hear his unnatural breathing. He would go into his and Mom's bedroom, and oh, how I hoped he would just go to sleep. Too many times he didn't.

Those were the worst. I would hear him and Mom fighting. Then he would storm back through the room and out the door, slamming it as he went. Ignition, the rev of a motor, and he was gone.

Somewhere deep within me now I hear a small voice that cries, "Daddy, please come back." Somewhere inside me is the three-year-old girl who wonders if Daddy will ever come back, who desperately wants someone to hold her and tell her that everything will be okay, who wails because her world is crumbling. But I don't remember ever consciously thinking that. It's all somewhere beyond memory.

How did I feel? Bad, that's all I knew. I don't remember ever crying. I only remember that everything within me just stopped. Froze. I felt dead inside.

What I believe now is that the fear of pain had begun tearing down the bridge between me and my dad. Between me and myself. It was the bridge of emotion, and I had started dismantling it piece by piece—pulling down the painful feelings I had toward him. The good feelings. *Any* feeling I had toward him. By the time of the divorce when I was seventeen, my bridge demolition was more or less finished. I felt indifferent.

Finally, was my only conscious thought.

But it's never that easy, and it's never final. When my mother had her first nervous breakdown a few months after the divorce, Dad came back drunk one evening and called all the kids into the living room. He told us Mom's condition was our fault. I only half believed him. Mostly, I just wanted him to leave. None of us ever talked about what he had said that night.

I was seventeen years old, and I had already ended my dad's life as far as I was concerned. He didn't exist for me emotionally. All his good traits—his humor, his charm, his beautiful singing voice (which by then was destroyed by emphysema)—none of it was available to me. It seemed appropriate that he had moved out of the house.

I didn't think I felt anything for my dad. But I used to. I remember running up the aisle at church right after the last "Amen," so that I wouldn't get caught in the crush of people. Then I could get to the choir loft and see Dad, and accompany him to the room where he changed his robe and talked and laughed with his friends. He was special. His tenor voice touched their hearts, my heart, with the songs of life, of heaven, of Jesus in the garden. I felt so alive with him then.

But all that changed. And it wasn't because he quit trying to love me. He was disabled, trapped in sin and disease. He never threw me out of his life. He kept making feeble attempts to cross the bridge, even when I didn't.

But the bridge was gone. And I didn't want it back. Not the good feelings, not the bad feelings, not any feelings.

No, I didn't think, *Daddy, please come back.* There was no way back. At least, I didn't think so then.

The influence of generations past, family patterns, and styles of relating all gather to make their impression on us as children. I've found that I didn't gain this stoic habit by accident. I have learned much from older family members about the qualities that have made my family strong—such as faith and perseverance—and I'm also learning other patterns that may not have served us well. I did not escape their impact on my life.

Rosemary, a lively, accomplished woman in her seventies, told me a story about how her mother modeled emotional restraint.

It was Sunday, during the early years of World War II. One week earlier, Rosemary's husband, Rob, had been killed in an airfield accident. Now Rosemary and her mother were sitting together in church, and the choir began to sing. Rosemary felt a strong urge to weep, and she started to get up and leave. But her mother took her hand, held it down, and gave her a steady look that said, "Be strong." So Rosemary swallowed her tears, and stayed.

Rosemary's mother was my grandmother. A faithful, dignified Christian lady, "Mammy" had seven children, one of whom is my mother. Mammy always stood erect and walked gracefully. She cared for and often helped our family, but she wasn't one to hold us grandchildren in her lap. Until the day of her death at ninety-four, she was a model of strength and faith.

In that story and others I get a glimpse into how the women in this family were guided to handle their painful emotions. I don't blame my grandmother, for she was only living out what had been modeled for her. What I learn from it is that my emotional habits are deeply ingrained in the fabric of family history, and that I shouldn't be surprised when I cling to them. But I know I can, by God's grace, discover them and trust His power to change them.

The message—that if we don't suppress deep pain we will be overwhelmed by it—has its roots in fear. In the face of such fear, denial becomes a survival mechanism. But as a Christian, I am realizing that denial hurts my relationship with the Lord and others. It is my fleshly way of handling the fear of strong feelings rather than trusting that God's presence, power, and compassion will keep me intact as the storm passes through.

How ironic that we who think we're strong because we "control" our emotions are not only hurting ourselves, but quenching the Holy Spirit in the process. We have simply exchanged one mistaken way of coping with painful feelings for another.

Roots of emotional repression. Although in Western society women have traditionally expressed their emotions more openly than men, in certain environments and situations even young girls can begin a pattern of suppressing emotion in order to adapt to life as it is.

Women who grew up in significantly dysfunctional families often experience a lack of emotional growth. Dr. Sandra Wilson describes what she calls emotional numbness:

I have counseled with many adults from alcoholic
families who keep smiling blandly even while they
describe scenes of incredible terror or deep pathos.
They have developed a kind of emotional leprosy.
Leprosy destroys the body's ability to register pain,
and growing up in alcoholic families often damages
the mind's ability to experience emotions.[4]

Dr. Wilson explains that the alcoholic family's unwritten
rules often allow the expression of neutral or pleasant
emotions, but show no tolerance for any kind of negative feelings such as anger or grief. It's not safe, these girls
learn, to be sad or mad in their world. So they numb their
feelings.

Without a healthy adult model, these daughters have
no idea they can express all their pain to the Lord or to an
understanding adult. Sadly, the family norms overshadow
the truth about God Himself.

But daughters of dysfunctional families aren't the only
ones. Girls who experience the breakdown of their parents'
marriage often suffer in a similar way. Norman Wright comments, "The pattern of daughters of divorce repressing their
emotions is prevalent." In *Always Daddy's Girl*, he deals with
the father's influence on his daughter's development. Since
girls often experience divorce as a kind of abandonment by
their fathers, he explains, a woman's emotional pattern may
be affected:

[The daughters] were angry at their fathers for abandoning them, but he wasn't available to be the target
of their anger. So a daughter often felt like venting
her anger on her mother, blaming her for the father's
absence. At the same time, the girl felt the need to
squelch her anger because Mom was all she had left,
and she needed her more than ever. . . . She [also]
feels the need to become an adult, filling the void
created by the missing father.[5]

So the young girl or teen stifles appropriate emotions and has to "grow up" too soon.

Another contributing cause of repression among daughters, according to Wright, stems from their perceptions of Mom's low self-esteem and their desire not to be identified with it. If Dad is viewed as strong and Mom as weak and "emotional," he explains, the girl will desire to emulate the "stronger" male patterns, which usually include emotional suppression. But what haunts me is that a cycle has locked in. Low self-esteem in mothers contributes to emotional repression in daughters, which, Carlson and others contend, contributes to low self-esteem in women.

How does emotional repression keep us from God's compassion? First, if we never feel our sadness, then we don't experience our need for comfort. For myself, I may know I'm feeling sad or angry, but I won't sit down and tell the Lord. I just don't. So I go around with grief and hostility inside that never get out, and then I'm a sitting duck for self-pity and depression.

I'm trying to recognize my feelings sooner, express them to the Lord or a loved one, believe and experience Jesus' compassion for me, and then either use their energy wisely or let them go.

The second reason that burying feelings prevents our being comforted is that our actions show that we may not *really* believe God's compassion is available. I may say that I think God's compassionate. I may read verses about it. But when I won't give myself permission to feel grief, I am signaling that I don't truly believe it's "kosher." God can't *really* feel sadness that way (because Dad didn't, or the pastor doesn't, and so on). God doesn't *really* feel with me. Really, He wants me to be strong—so okay, I will be. That's what I do best.

How easily I forget that God is not interested in what I do best, but in my receiving what *He* does best! In this case, His best is sympathizing and comforting. "As a father has compassion on his children, so the LORD has compassion on those who fear him," proclaims the psalmist (103:13). Part of fearing the Lord is believing how tender He is toward his children who hurt, when they turn to Him.

Shame on You

This pattern of repression leads us into the second obstacle to experiencing more of God's tender compassion: the *problem of shame*, which we also talked about as a source of silent pain in chapter two. According to psychologists, shame can either be true and appropriate (what we call guilt), or false and inappropriate. Appropriate shame is simply the true guilt we feel when we have done something we identify as wrong or displeasing to God. This feeling helps us notice the problem and take steps to remedy it. Even secularists believe temporary, appropriate shame or guilt is necessary to personal health.

But shame becomes an obstacle to feeling God's compassion when we have a chronic, general sense of being worth less than others. Sandra Wilson perceptively describes shame:

> Whereas guilt is a feeling that "I have done something bad," shame is a feeling that "I *am* something bad." Guilt is a matter of behavior. Shame is a matter of identity. . . . Shame is the soul-deep feeling of being fatally flawed, less than—and apart from—other human beings. . . . "I have to try twice as hard to be half as good as other people."[6]

For the Christian, Wilson pinpoints the difference between knowing I am a sinner and feeling false shame: the sense that I am, in my essence, *worse* than other sinners. This feeling may drive us to perform compulsively or to give up altogether, Wilson explains, but it seldom draws us to the grace of God. And it keeps us from God's compassion because we think we don't deserve it.

It's important to note that the biblical concept that we

are sinners in need of grace can be a source of shame tem-
porarily, *until* we accept the grace of God in Jesus Christ for
salvation from shame. But then its work is done. Chronic
shame has no place in the heart of a Christian. If we give
it a place, it leads us to legalism—a spiritual compulsion
to perform for approval. Because there is no condemnation
in Christ, I shouldn't accept chronic shame as a legitimate
feeling.

Among other causes of this soul-sickness, parental neglect
is often cited as one culprit. According to Wright, even well-
meaning parents, despite their best efforts, can sometimes
neglect their daughter's basic needs for time, attention, and
direction. As a result, she feels abandoned emotionally. She
may grow up feeling that her basic needs do not deserve
to be met and that she doesn't deserve to be nurtured.
Therefore, a sense of incompleteness or immaturity lingers
within her soul, and the adult woman feels responsible for
and ashamed of her condition. As one friend described it,
"One of my biggest shame-producing thoughts in life is that
I'm causing all my own misery and therefore God isn't going
to let Himself be pulled down into it with me."

So when we feel ashamed of feeling this way, Wright
explains, we often cover up the mess with a false maturity:

> Shame flaws the real you so that just trying to be
> yourself is painful. So in order to survive the pain you
> develop a false self, a defensive mask which is used to
> hide from yourself and others all the pain and loneli-
> ness you feel.[7]

This pattern explains why the daughters (and sons) of
such home environments often *look* so good. And, certainly,
some do survive and thrive better than others. But the shame
problem can motivate the over-achiever as well as the under-
achiever, only with different effects.

But if women who suffer this inadequacy ever quit
over-achieving (or over-eating, over-loving, over-spending,

or over-anything that numbs their souls) and start feeling silent pain, shame can make them feel they don't deserve to be comforted or supported. They've been earning approval for so long — from parents, teachers, bosses — that they can't tolerate feeling needy. That feeling is associated with shame, and they can't believe anyone could tolerate, much less have compassion for, their inner pain. Not even God.

I've felt that way. Those were the times when I couldn't reconcile God's allowing the pain with the idea that He suffers with me. If I feel the slightest shame that I deserve this oppressive pain or that I "shouldn't" need comfort, then my false guilt smothers my ability to feel God's sympathy.

What I now want to tell myself — and you, if you're in this dilemma — is this: *Dear one, there is no condemnation, no shame in Christ Jesus. Resist the temptation to keep reviewing your actions like instant replays and just run to Him. Let go of your performance and look to a Person. Make Him your hiding place. See how He identifies with you in your pain, even your emotional pain over the way your friends are forsaking you. Pour out your anguish of soul, not in bickering over your performance, but in the baring of your pain-filled heart. He hears you. He longs to hold you in the arms of His Spirit as you cry to Him. Jesus is waiting inside those dark, closed rooms within. When you enter in faith, you'll find Him there.*

"The Lord draws near to the broken-hearted" (Psalm 34:18). When your mind wants to bargain, let your heart break.

Sin and Compassion

We've looked at false shame. But what about deliberate sin in our life, which produces true guilt? Isn't that final obstacle to comfort one that the Lord erects? Can we experience His compassion when we are in the midst of *known, unconfessed sin*?

Probably the clearest verse on this question is Proverbs 28:13 — "He who conceals his transgressions will not prosper, but he who confesses and forsakes them will find compassion" (NASB). This proverb emphasizes the bad results we suffer when we hide our sin, and the benefits we gain by confessing it.

That's exactly the opposite of the way we think. I usually consider all the penalties for owning up to my mistakes and concentrate on the benefits of concealing them. But the Lord, as usual, turns things upside down.

God looks at this from the perspective of what is best for us. When we are learning and generally obeying, things may go fairly well. But if we stumble into sin and then, even after gentle nudging from the Holy Spirit, we won't let go of it, the Lord often allows painful consequences that will turn us back to Him. When we're knowingly and stubbornly clinging to actions clearly contrary to Scripture, things we may have been repeatedly convicted about, we "do not prosper." Why? Because the Lord loves us too ferociously to let us go on destroying ourselves. Brennan Manning describes this ferocious protectiveness:

> The Lion who will kill all that separates us from
> Him; the Lamb who was killed to mend that sepa-
> ration—both are symbols and synonyms for Jesus.
> Relentlessness and tenderness; indivisible aspects of
> the Divine Reality.[8]

Isaiah had an intimate acquaintance with these dimensions of God's character as he watched his people enduring the painful consequences of hundreds of years of disobedience and known, unconfessed sin. The Lord had warned them again and again, but they wouldn't listen. He waited patiently, desiring them to heed His prophets and give up their self-defeating idolatry.

This is how God as Lion finally confronted them with His love:

> By warfare and exile [God contends] with her—
>   with his fierce blast he drives her out,

> as on a day the east wind blows. . . .
> When he makes all the altar stones [for idols]
>   to be like chalk stones crushed to pieces.
>   (27:8-9)

In His relentless love, the Holy One of Israel would not allow His people to continue indefinitely dishonoring Him and destroying themselves. As He grieved over their self-destructive behaviors, His discipline involved *removing* their comfort, driving them out of their land, and smashing the idols they had trusted for security. In His ferocious love and faithfulness, He removed their experience of His compassion:

> For this is a people without understanding;
>   so their Maker has no compassion on them,
>   and their Creator *shows* them no favor. (27:11)

But behind the tough discipline lingered the heart of love and the deep desire to bless. It was His intense, compassionate desire for Israel's deliverance from ultimate pain that motivated the loving Lion of Judah to turn them from their path of self-destruction. During all the discipline Isaiah warned about, he reassured them of the Lord's eventual plan for their restoration. Even while the Lord appeared to be most harsh, Isaiah said in a hundred ways, "Yet the LORD longs to be gracious to you; *he rises to show you compassion*" (30:18; emphasis added).

How amazing that God never stops longing to be gracious. His compassions never fail, but He may stop *showing* us His compassion. Yet in all our afflictions, He is afflicted. He never stops grieving for us, even when His face toward us is stern.

Can we ever believe that behind even the painful consequences of our sinful choices lies the suffering sympathy of a God who doesn't want us to continue abusing ourselves? In His compassion, He withdraws our sense of His love only in order to drive us to a helpless surrender—and back into the comfort of His compassion.

All He asks of us is confession, not a self-reformed life.

Only three verses before Isaiah's declaration of God's longing to have compassion, the Lord gives us the remedy for our self-inflicted pain: "In repentance and rest is your salvation, in quietness and trust is your strength" (30:15).

Biblical repentance is a healthy kind of burnout, an acute awareness that I can't manage the problem any longer and I need God's power. When I repent, I realize that I am utterly helpless to change. It's no accident that the highly effective Twelve-Step program, which is derived from Christian principles, begins with this helplessness in Step One: "We admitted that we were powerless and that our lives had become unmanageable."

Simply confessing our wrong before God and trusted people, turning to the Lord with a quiet trust—not earning our way back into His favor—is our rescue from the silent pain caused by sin.

Israel wouldn't receive the rest God offered. Will I? Will you? We don't have to carry the sin or its pain. In the greatest act of compassion in all history, Jesus did that already. Isaiah prophesied how the Savior would make it possible for us to lay down the weight of sin and its pain. He let Himself be pulled down into it with us:

> But he was pierced for our transgressions,
>   he was crushed for our iniquities;
> the punishment that brought us peace was upon him,
>   and by his wounds we are healed. (53:5)

If you're feeling crushed by self-destructive patterns and guilt-producing habits, Someone is offering you a rescue. The pain you're feeling is not a curse, but an evidence that the Lord still longs to show you compassion, because the pain means that He is still trying to draw you back.

If you're in silent pain because of sin, take heart. The

worst curse of all is when the Lord allows your heart to become so emotionless that you don't feel the pain anymore. Take heart, because the Man of sorrows has known, and feels with you now, *even the pain of discipline,* for "God made him who had no sin to be sin for us" (2 Corinthians 5:21).

Take heart, dear one: the pain itself is allowed by the compassion of our God, who longs for your heart to be His, who is at work in your life to make you whole.

7

How God Reaches Us in Our Silence

ॐ

If we're tuned to epiphanies —
those guiding flashes of sacred insight —
they happen, usually just when
we need them most.[1]

SUE MONK KIDD

When Brian was three years old, his serious breathing problems due to a brainstem cyst meant that he would need neurosurgery in Houston. Every time he inhaled, we heard an audible gasp. His vocal cords were gradually becoming paralyzed because of the cyst's pressure on vital nerves. Without an operation, the problem would only get worse.

But even after successful surgery, Brian came home with a tracheostomy. At three, he faced another disability: the at-least-temporary inability to eat or talk, two of his favorite things. The possibility of permanent dependence on this artificial tube seemed like more than we could bear.
Faithful Christians gathered to pray for Brian just before we left for Houston. As the fifteen or so others sat in a circle in our friends' living room, one after the other prayed for Brian's healing and strength for us. When I tried to pray, I could only cry and struggle to give thanks that a "trake" could save Brian's life. But in the middle of that painful

evening, one friend's ministry touched me with God's compassion like nothing else.

Inez had been a speech therapist for years. She had seen firsthand the disabling effects of a trake, especially in children. She had labored to help them learn to talk, observed the complications that can arise, and become familiar with the cumbersome and tedious care necessary to ensure safety and health. She knew Brian—how much he loved to talk and sing Christian songs, what a loss he would suffer if the trake became permanent.

That night during prayer, Inez began to weep with me. Not hysterically, but audibly. She let the full impact of Brian's situation break her heart. She had seen the experience of others and probably knew the trial ahead better than we did. Because she shared our reality, she was able to share our sorrow. And with that courage to feel the pain, she channeled God's living compassion to my heart through her tears.

Somehow, I could trust God's love a little more because I *heard* His heart break with ours—through one of His children. Because of Inez's willingness to weep, I could *feel* the Lord's compassion, and it soothed and strengthened me, because I no longer felt so alone.

Inez wasn't the only one. While I was in Houston, on separate occasions, good friends left home and family and drove four hours to be with me during that draining hospital experience. Trisha and Elaine took me to their motel room one night where they prayed and let me just cry. Later, Donna and Marion came, bringing the comfort of their presence and companionship. Each of these expressions of compassion (of simply being with me in the pain) helped me to endure without losing faith in God's love—because I could see compassion in their eyes.

BREAKING THE SURFACE OF SILENT PAIN

What do these stories about crisis pain have to do with silent pain? Simply this: When silent pain takes us back into those dark, abandoned rooms of our souls, the grief, pain, and anger we encounter may send us into a temporary crisis. Those doors weren't slammed shut in the first place over minor irritations. They were slammed on major heartbreaks and lingering losses. And when we ask the Lord to bring His light and love into our innermost being, we often find hiding there a deep sadness or rage. We are reentering a mourning process that was never completed.

In a sense, we are resurfacing pain and bringing it to the resurrection power and presence of the Christ within us. His presence can soothe our hearts with the deepest sympathy we have ever known, and His power can change our sinful responses to the pain. But just as in any crisis, we need the active support of friends, and we can discover other creative ways the Lord may magnify His compassion in our hearts.

Empty Words and Echoes

As many saints have testified, in times of deep grief Scripture may often sound like a cacaphony of empty words; prayer, like a canyon bouncing back echoes.

When I first encountered the darkness of the abandoned rooms of my soul, I clung to the promises of God's sovereignty, which kept me from despair. But I *felt* very little comfort from the words of Scripture. I believed in my mind that God was compassionate, but I didn't *experience* His comfort through spiritual communion. This didn't mean I would abandon these disciplines, only add to them.

That's when the Father of all comfort graciously began to open my eyes, ears, and senses and to communicate His tender heart in ways I could hear, see, and feel. That evening in prayer with our friends, I heard Inez crying. Other times, I looked into loved ones' eyes or I felt their embrace.

The Lord often reaches our spirit through our senses. John proclaimed the evidence of God's revelation in Christ, which they had *heard, seen,* and *touched* (1 John 1:1). Learning experts tell us that we learn best if we use all three channels for taking in data: auditory, visual, and kinesthetic.

God's people, who share Christ's nature, are the most vibrant reflections of His heart. But they weren't the only expression of compassion to my senses in those times of emotional numbness. As I stumbled forward in faith, God's compassion slowly sounded, appeared, and brushed against me—through music, imagery, and nature. But since people express Him most fully, I want to begin there.

GOD'S PEOPLE: THE FACE OF HIS COMPASSION

When I began to enter the abandoned rooms in my mansion, I needed the same kind of loving support we received when Brian went through crisis. As I discovered my hidden sadness and rage, I was given the opportunity to change my old responses to the pain from self-protection to love. Mark Lloyd Taylor refers to this confrontation as a necessary stewardship: "We need to be stewards of our pain . . . we must neither deny the pain nor get caught in it, but rather work through it to find life on the other side."[2]

For me, part of that stewardship was "finishing" my grief inside the warmth of God's compassion, which helped me turn away from the sinful patterns I had developed to protect myself from my dad and from the family's pain. I needed to forgive from my heart and emotions, not just from my mind, as I had for so long.

Another part of that stewardship was asking the Lord for others who could share the reality of my sadness, just as Inez had shared the reality of our pain over Brian. Those who can sympathize are able to reflect God's compassion to us, just as we can reflect it for them. I believe that's why He asks us to "weep with those who weep" (and the reason for tears seems to make no difference) because Jesus Christ wants His Body on earth to be an audible, visible expression of His compassion.

Kneading and Feeding

In order to comfort each other with the compassion we have received from God, we must share our personal stories. The

Bible itself is a storybook, echoing throughout the generations the common experience of human beings and the immutability of God.

In "The Story-Shaped Life," Sue Monk Kidd writes of the importance of telling our personal story, of entering into it ourselves with boldness so we may find its meaning, the true meaning that Christ alone has given it:

> To fashion an inner story of our pain carries us into
> the heart of it, which is where rebirth inevitably
> occurs. Telling our story puts us in an inner room
> with our suffering and allows us to dialogue with
> it in God's presence, to reinterpret it in the light of
> God's participation. God enables us to see our diffi-
> culty in a new context and thereby find the comfort
> and courage to live it. . . . *The inner tale transforms by
> reorienting us to new truth and insight, breaking open the
> hidden holy that dwells in our experience.*[3]

This dialogue she describes is not something we can do easily in a vacuum. "Breaking open the hidden holy" in our lives often begins with pain, for which we need comfort. It continues with insight, which we often gain from hearing others' stories. And it comes to resolution (although not perfectly) as we reinterpret our past in light of God's love, for which we need encouragement from others who are on the same path.

Unfortunately, I had never found this kind of opportunity within the walls of a church. But I did find it within the Body of Christ through the informal ministry of my friend Frances Swann. With others who were ready to grow by entering their personal story, I found safety, comfort, and a sharing of burdens that I had never known before. I felt nourished in a hungry part of my soul. I felt emotionally fed. Sue Monk Kidd describes how this happens:

> Ideally, the congregation is a place where believers
> offer their joys, wounds, and journeys to one another.

Ultimately, we knead our stories into bread in order
to feed one another. When we share our inner stories,
we allow others to enter our lives and partake of our
deepest truths.[4]

This kind of place where we "knead our stories into
bread" is not something for which the church has traditionally made room. Women's ministries often center on
Bible study, prayer groups, and missionary committees,
which are all needed. But many churches have not provided
an appropriate context for healing the kinds of emotional
struggles so common today.

For lack of a better term, I call this model that I saw
in my friend's ministry a "Christian spiritual/emotional
growth group." The group was Christ-centered. From the
first day on we stressed that only the Lord, in the quiet times
we spent with Him in thought and prayer, could change our
hearts. His Word was our strength, and other materials were
useful (which I will describe elsewhere). Also, each of us
committed ourselves to pray for each member of the group
every day.

This group wasn't a Bible study or a teaching format
of any kind. It was designed to deal with personal spiritual and emotional issues because these are often more
consciously intertwined for women. With our greater needs
for conversation, active listening, openness and honesty, and
emotional intimacy women benefit greatly from this kind of
fellowship—especially when dealing with silent pain. The
traditional prayer group, understandably, doesn't have the
time or guidelines for this kind of ministry.

Most important for me, I felt safe with this group. We
stressed the importance of confidentiality, and we committed to be there every week, barring something unavoidable.
This gave the group stability and security.

Another part of the safety was emotional. *All* my feelings were accepted. The atmosphere Frances set was one in
which our emotions could be felt and expressed (we went

through at least a dozen boxes of tissues) but not directed at maligning someone else. Talking about how we *felt* when someone did or said something, while focusing on ourselves and not the other person, kept us from placing blame on others. Simple acknowledgment of the offense or pain didn't imply criticism of the other person. And where sins were suffered, forgiveness as the goal was always assumed.

But in the meantime, it was enormously healing just to have the opportunity to talk about my fear, grief, anger, and guilt—or say things I had never said—without someone trying to pacify, qualify, amend, contradict, or solve. Our group did not view negative emotions as "bad."

Evelyn Bassoff, therapist and author, tells how she invites her clients to see themselves as the host or hostess of a banquet. To this banquet, they are to invite all their emotions, not excluding any of them, and let them each have a respected place at the table. If any of them are left out, she explains, they will become unruly and act up in one way or another until they gain the attention they have been denied.

One of the blessings of having Christian friends around as I struggled with these feelings was seeing the Lord's compassion through them. I knew He was a God of compassion, but sometimes I needed to see it in their eyes, hear it in their voices, and feel it in their hugs. Or I needed to sense it simply in their presence as I talked, discovering that they still accepted me when I had talked it out.

In this quiet refuge of the soul, *I felt secure enough to listen to the Christ within*—who gently corrected me or trained my heart in new directions. All of us have been wounded and are guilty of wounding others, but the kindness of God's compassion for my wounds led me to the deep repentance of wanting with all my heart to please Him who loves me so tenderly.

I took with me from this group *the permanent gift of God's compassion mediated through His people,* just as Frances did for me later. I can put that experience on the face of the Lord. As I internalized His compassion—digested the "bread" in

my own heart—I became more able to experience His comforting presence even when others weren't around.

That growing fullness has opened up to me *the joy of
showing compassion to others* as I let them partake of Christ's
sympathy in my life. As Scripture tells us, we can comfort
others only *after* we have received the comfort of the Lord
ourselves.

That's what these groups have done for me. They have
given me an emotional refuge, a place of healing through
experiencing and then internalizing God's compassion, and
the opportunity to let Christ's comforting presence in me
offer comfort to others.

Some people I talk to wonder how this kind of group
can escape being dragged down into the depressing dol-
drums of hearing so much heartache. My experience was
quite the opposite (although there are pitfalls, which I'll turn
to in chapter nine).

I found that bearing each other's burdens was an
easy yoke to put on. That's in part because in our group,
laughter was as common as weeping. Sometimes I laughed
because I identified hilariously with something someone
else described. It was an expression of relief that I wasn't
alone. But even in the midst of tears, it wasn't unusual for
the person sharing to make a funny remark. Sometimes
levity came from relief over finally being able to speak the
emotional truth, sometimes from a renewed perspective, but
always from an open heart. I believe that when we're free
to feel our sorrow, we are freer to feel our joy. Donald W.
McCullough writes,

> The paradox is this: Great mourners are great
> rejoicers. In opening the door to pain, they also
> open it to joy. People who do not mourn, who
> slam the door on all sorrow, never feel the deepest
> delights. Their lives, like freeways on which they
> speed from one entertaining distraction to another,
> are too hard for anything but the most superficial

pleasures to pass over. But those sensitive enough
to be crushed by sadness are those who also can be
lifted by happiness.[5]

Another liberating aspect of the group was that no one
felt responsible for anyone else. We were responsible *to* each
other—to pray and respond with grace and compassion, but
not to heal. We weren't there to cure or control, but to pour
out our hearts and have the joy of watching the Lord do the
work in our lives.

To me, that's one advantage of a small group over a
single friend: no one person feels the whole weight of the
problem. In a group, it's as if each one has laid her bur-
den out in the middle, and the others show acceptance and
compassion, but together we entrust the "solution"—or the
waiting when there's no solution—to the Lord. Bearing one
another's burdens by faith, as a group, wasn't oppressive
for me.

The friends in these groups, of course, aren't the only
people who reflect God's compassion. God also does it
through spouses, family, friends, pastors, and counselors
in informal ways.

Mary, my friend whose father left when she was three,
described her husband's compassion as she battled with
agoraphobia, depression, and hospitalization:

> Steve continually affirmed my worth and value, and he
> believed in me—the "core" me. Even when I couldn't
> perform and I wasn't my usual self, it was as if he
> could see through to the real Mary, and he com-
> municated unconditional compassion and love that
> way. All this helped to allay my deep fear of being
> abandoned.

But people, as wonderful as they are, haven't been the
only channel the Lord has used to convey His compassion.
People aren't always perfect reflections of His heart, or they

aren't always available, or they aren't able to embody all that He wants to show us about Himself. For these reasons, the Lord wants us to enjoy many other sounds, sights, and strokes of comfort—if only we have the ears to hear, the eyes to see, and the hands to feel.

MUSIC: THE MELODIES OF GOD'S COMPASSION

For a month after I was diagnosed with multiple sclerosis, I was having difficulty feeling anything. I was awkward around others because I didn't know how I felt, and I found myself almost wanting them to tell me how I should feel, or to feel my sadness for me. I was paralyzed with emotional shock.

One day, as I was driving home from taking Brian to school, I heard a song on our local Christian radio station that finally brought down my emotional walls. I remember listening to it while sitting at a red light, tears flooding my eyes until I could barely see to drive. The song is called "You'll See a Man," by Harvest, and I bought and played the song many times during those days. The refrain called me to see Jesus as a human being who shared my pain:

> You'll see a Man acquainted with your sorrow.
> You'll see His eyes sharing in your tears.
> You'll see His arms never lost their hold on you.
> Lift your eyes, you'll see a Man.[6]

The thought that Jesus shared my tears had occurred to me before, but hearing those words set to music suddenly made the truth come alive. Over that next year, as the Lord used music to touch my heart, I put together about thirty selections on a tape I made for myself and entitled "His Compassions." Whenever I feel the need to be comforted, I listen. I see His eyes. I feel His arms. In fact, I notice that many of the songs I chose have lyrics about physical touch: "leaning on the everlasting arms," "Lord, take my hand," "I want to let Jesus love me, put His arms around me."

When Paul encouraged the Ephesians to share psalms, hymns, and spiritual songs with one another, he was prescribing a balm for those of us in silent pain. And as I listen, I give thanks that I have a God so compassionate that he pours His comfort through music, so that we can hear the tender melodies of His compassion.

The Unique Power of Music

By God's design, music can pierce our inner walls and reach the abandoned rooms in the mansion of our soul with an almost mystical comfort and power.

I was poignantly reminded of this as I read William Styron's *Darkness Visible,* an exquisite account of the award-winning novelist's battles with deep depression.

On the night Styron was deliberately preparing to take his own life, he described how he sat in his living room and inexplicably forced himself to watch an old movie in which a friend played a small part. At one point in the film, the characters were walking down the halls of a music conservatory, and from behind the walls an unseen woman sang a passage from Brahms' *Alto Rhapsody*:

> This sound, which like all music—indeed, like all
> pleasure—I had been numbly unresponsive to for
> months, pierced my heart like a dagger, and in a
> flood of swift recollection I thought of all the joys
> the house had known; the children who had rushed
> through its rooms, the festivals, the love and work,
> the honestly earned slumber, the voices and nimble
> commotion. . . . All this I realized was more than
> I could ever abandon, even as what I had set out so
> deliberately to do was more than I could inflict on those
> memories, and upon those, so close to me, with whom
> the memories were bound. And just as powerfully I
> realized I could not commit this desecration on myself.[7]

Just exactly how the Lord changed William Styron's intentions through music, I will never know. But in the final pages of his book, the author writes that one source of his lifelong battle with depression was unresolved grief over his mother's death when he was thirteen. And yet, as Styron explains, she ironically played a role in his rescue:

> My own avoidance of death may have been belated homage to my mother. I do know that in those last hours before I rescued myself, when I listened to the passage from the *Alto Rhapsody — which I'd heard her sing* — she had been very much on my mind.[8]

Part of music's power is that it carries messages through three different senses — hearing, visualizing (through word pictures in the lyrics), and feeling responses to the melody itself. But here, Styron describes the power of music to wrap itself around important people in our lives and revitalize emotional connections with them. For him, it formed a connection with life-giving, motherly comfort that coaxed him back from the brink of suicide.

IMAGES: THE PICTURES OF GOD'S COMPASSION

For all of us, but especially for visually oriented people, pictures are worth pages of words. That's why even in literature and oratory, word pictures, metaphors, illustrations, and stories are essential to communicating well. Good poetry almost requires an image to bring it to life, to give it a visual dimension, and to make it convincing. Abstract concepts are always easier to grasp when we translate them into concrete examples from nature or life.

No one did this better than Jesus, the greatest teacher. Everywhere He looked Jesus saw and used analogies to explain Himself: bread, grapevines, water, farmers, shepherds, seeds, coins, servants, lilies, birds, even mother hens. Scripture is filled with images in the poetry of the Psalms and prophets (such as the mother-imagery God used to describe Himself) as well as in the prose of the gospels and epistles.

As believers, we have the mind of Christ, the Creator of all these images. Indwelt by His Spirit, we have a divine interpreter who can touch our emotions and apply the practical principles we gain from visual images. Even more than the secularists who don't share these advantages, we can enjoy imagery to its fullest.

Spirit-Inspired Imaging

It bothers me that this rich gift is being threatened today by fears of the worldly emphasis on "imaging" that we hear about in the so-called New Age movement. Because this misguided movement has abused human imagination to guide people into unhealthy fantasy in the name of truth-seeking, some Christians seem to react by throwing out the baby with the bath water (a trite but horrifying image, if you think about it).

I looked up the word *imaging* one day and found that it simply means "calling up a mental picture of." Like every other human capacity, I realized, it can be used or abused. The problem isn't the process of imaging, but the motivation and the purpose for which it's used.

In Psalm 23, David was imaging. Based on his rich experience as a shepherd, this songwriter called up a mental picture of a shepherd and began letting that image illustrate God's character, which he knew from Scripture. Every action—his leading to quiet streams, his provision of nurture and safety—had visual pictures and emotional overtones to secure them in David's mind and heart. That is the power of imaging in the context of revealed truth about God's character: It allows us to experience through our senses the reality of our God who is pure Spirit.

So rather than throw out imaging due to fear, we can let the Lord use it to its fullest in our hearts as we are guided by His Word and His Spirit. Rather than run from such a powerful gift, we can take it captive (or recapture it) so that it can serve Christ. Because we have the incredible privilege of having the mind of Christ and His truth, we Christians have the greatest capacity for the most glorious use of this God-given potential.

For experiencing God's compassion, I like to picture the Lord holding, comforting, and affirming me the way I do my own sons. (Or the way I see other parents who do it.) That's no different, it seems to me, than what David did in Psalm 23. He projected his own shepherding experience onto his view of God, because the very idea of a good shepherd (or a good-enough mother) comes from His common grace in the first place.

My husband, who is an internal medicine physician, tries to keep his fingertips from becoming calloused so that they remain sensitive. As he examines patients, he uses his sense of touch to help him "see" beneath the skin, to find anything that might be harmful to the patient. Lloyd's sensitive hands remind me that God's probing within me is gentle, and that His purpose is to find and treat something that may harm me. I learned that from Scripture, but I can feel it when I touch Lloyd's hands.

Spiritual imaging is not casting God in my image, but merely seeing His reflection in what He has made. It enhances my mental understanding by enabling me to feel the emotional associations connected with word pictures.

Images and Intimacy
Because images carry these emotional overtones, I've found that they can also enhance intimacy. David used imagery in the psalms not only to describe God, but also to describe his own thoughts and feelings, and it enriched his (and our) communication and intimacy with the Lord. "As the deer pants for streams of water, so my soul pants for you, O God" (Psalm 42:1). "I am forgotten by [friends] as though I were dead; I have become like broken pottery" (Psalm 31:12).

One day when I was feeling especially confused and

sad, I remember throwing myself down on the bed and telling the Lord that I was holding my soul up to Him like a little child would bring a broken toy to a loving father. In a few simple words, I had opened my heart in dependence and trust, and because of the image, I felt more sure that the Lord looked at me with fatherly affection and sympathy. The word picture also encouraged my own childlike faith that my heavenly Father could and would fix my brokenness.

NATURE: A HANDS-ON MUSEUM OF COMPASSION

When I was pregnant with Brian, Lloyd and I had the opportunity to visit San Diego for several days while he attended a conference. We stayed in a beautiful motel that opened onto the gentle, quiet shoreline of Mission Bay.

With the "waves" of pregnancy hormones washing over my sometimes grumpy self, one morning I had been pretty testy before Lloyd left for his meeting. After an interesting day of whale-watching (which reminded me of myself taking a bath), I took a walk on the shoreline and began feeling convicted of my irascibility that morning, especially since we were in such a pleasant vacation spot.

As I kicked off my shoes and waded, enjoying the sparkling sunlight on the water, I received a gift of communion with the Lord, an inexplicable encounter with grace that I recorded in these words:

> Late afternoon, I walk barefoot
> on the shores of Mission Bay.
> Quiet inland sea in gentle ripples
> wraps silence over my soul,
> as dark sand and watery clay
> soil these traveler feet.
>
> Though guilt, like gravity, protests,
> He kneels and draws a rising wave
> to wash them clean again,

then wipes them with the breeze
that girds Him
and gazes at me from sea's golden surface
with His sun-jeweled eyes.

With this unbidden, soothing reminder of my cleansing—
and how regularly and rhythmically God's love washes over
me—I felt my heart soften toward Lloyd. When we were
together again, my apology was lighthearted. I felt whole
and new.

God's creation, too, washes over us regularly and rhythmically with His glory and loveliness. The testimony of
Scripture to God's character guides us in interpreting the
beauties of nature, correcting whatever distortions our human
understanding may introduce. With the guideline that my
interpretations must not contradict the written word, I am
free to listen to the myriad ways the Living Word speaks
to me in the artistry of earth, sky, seas, and wind. Oswald
Chambers writes,

> In every wind that blows, in every night and day of
> the year, in every sign of the sky, in every blossoming
> and in every withering of the earth, there is a real
> coming of God to us if we will simply use our imagi-
> nation to realize it.[9]

Creation as Comfort

Poet Luci Shaw has published excerpts from her journal during the two years before and after losing her husband to
cancer. In *God in the Dark*, Luci (who has since remarried)
recounts the days of her grief and struggle over the sick-
ness and eventual death of Harold Shaw, then-president of
Harold Shaw Publishers.

One recurring element in her writing is the place that
Creation—its sights, sounds, and suggestions—played in
her wrestling with loss. Also an amateur photographer, Luci
often went for walks or drives with her camera in order to

capture God's artistry and self-revelation.

This poet, to whom words are treasured friends, describes that in her grief she was without words from God that could reach her heart. She writes of the silence and the darkness that often envelops even the most spiritual man or woman during grief. In that thick darkness of mourning, she focused her eyes on the Word-made-wood in the meadows, made-ice on quiet streams, and made-silk in milkweed pods. She found a subtle comfort there:

> Have matted two prints for friends: the burst milk-weed pod with seeds and silk silhouetted in light, and the two fallen elderberry leaves caught in the ice the night the temperature dropped. It has been one of my perceptions this year that the beauty of Creation suffuses even decay and death—the *fallen* leaf, the fragile, *shattered* shell of ice, the *frozen* stream, the *burst* pod.[10]

As she connects the icy frost of winter with her loss, she describes a slide she took of ice crystals on a window pane with an orange sky in the background:

> Somehow there's an attention-getting incongru-ity—the remote, enormous incandescence of the sun in service to these small, pale, cold fragments of frost, the permanent illuminating the transient, power caressing fragility, the interplay of far and near kiss-ing on the window before my eyes. This could be a metaphor for God's reaching to humankind to bathe them in brightness . . . or to take them home to heaven.[11]

Sue Monk Kidd has also touched my life with the healing power of God's creation. In her book *When the Heart Waits,* she perceptively describes the spiritual jour-ney through her own mid-life transformation. As she was taking a walk one winter day, feeling the cold deadness of her spirit, she stumbled onto a message in the bare limbs of a tree.

> I burrowed into the wind, my head down. I happened to look up again as I passed beneath the branches of a dogwood tree, and my eyes fell upon a curious little appendage suspended from a twig just over my head.
>
> I kept walking. *No, stop . . . look closer.* Not knowing what else to do but obey the inner impulse, I backed up and looked again. I took one step toward it, then two, until I was so close that the fog of my breath encircled it. *I had come upon a cocoon.*
>
> I was caught suddenly by a sweep of reverence, by a sensation that made me want to sink to my knees. For somehow I knew that I had stumbled upon an epiphany, a strange gracing of my darkness.[12]

The author lets this reminder of rebirth, this simple cocoon, become a positive symbol amid her confusion:

> During the days after my February walk, I asked myself what would happen if I could learn the spiritual art of cocooning. Might I discover a stilling of the soul that invites God and a new recreation of life? Would I see that waiting, with all its quiet passion and hidden fire, is the real crucible of spiritual transformation?[13]

That encounter with nature became a guiding image in her own transformation and in her message of comfort and hope to others.

Celebrate the Simple

Not all our experiences of God's comfort through nature are dramatic epiphanies. Just celebrating the simple joys of God's earth can soothe the soul. Walking through the woods or down the block, gazing at the stars or listening to a bubbling stream, can become an encounter with the Lord's compassion if I'm looking for it.

I have found comfort in seeing and touching the firm, comfortable "cradle" of a mockingbird's nest a friend brought to our sons. I love to take a fallen rose petal and stroke it against my cheek. Although it may happen, we don't have to find a "principle" in order to be soothed by God's world.

My friend Linda told me that when she was a young girl, she read in Psalms that God's faithfulness to David's family line would be like "the moon, the faithful witness in the sky" (89:37). From then on, whenever she saw the moon, Linda said she thought of God's faithfulness to her.

"The times I remember most were when I was a young mother and would be up at night with crying babies," she recalled. "That can be a very lonely time. When I saw the moon, it would be a comforting reminder that the Lord was faithful, that He would be 'up' with me."

Why the moon, Lord? I thought. Later, it occurred to me that the moon is not only dependable, but it is also visible evidence during the darkness that the sun still shines. In our emotionally dark nights, the Lord sends small reflections to reassure us that the "Son" of God's love still shines.

I love to walk at sunset. Where I grew up in West Texas, wide-open sunsets were some of the few beautiful sights nature offered in that parched area. Perhaps not only their beauty, but also their connection to my childhood, have created a special place in my heart for God's evening "light shows."

My response to this daily grace has always been tranquility, quiet comfort, and reflection. Not until recently had I thought through the beauty to one of its many messages.

Sunset provides the only opportunity to look directly at the sun, because its blinding "glory" is clothed in the cumulative dust of the earth's atmosphere. We see its shape. We watch it splash the sky with color and outline the clouds with silver and gold. Veiled in dust, the dying sun lends heaven its deepest brilliance. And the idle rhythm of day's end offers me time to ponder the compassion of this "incarnation."

Now I live in a city of trees and hills that block most of the horizon at twilight. As a result, not many people in the city watch the sunsets here. There is one high point in our neighborhood that I look forward to reaching on my walks because I get a better view of the sky. But whether I'm there to watch His artistry or not, the Lord puts on His "light show" every evening, even though it plays to a small crowd, then quietly folds up His wares and travels on down the road.

One morning at church, a good friend who lives on a nearby lake started telling me about the evening skies she and her husband enjoy from their deck. Her eyes grew wide and bright with the thrill of what she was recalling. Then she bubbled, "And when the sun goes down, the show is just getting started!"

How true, I thought. When the Son went down, the show was just getting started.

What else but gracious, humble compassion would stoop each day to soothe our overstressed, emotional lives with a tranquil reminder of incarnation and resurrection? Whether we ever see it or not.

February in the Garden

Of course, the experience of God's compassion is a gift from Him, not something we can earn or produce, even by our fervent prayers. Finally, we are dependent. And that means that sometimes we enter seasons of waiting on God.

In our area, late March and early April are the glorious times when dogwood trees and azaleas in twenty different shades of pink, red, and white bloom everywhere. Our community has marked Azalea Trail with signs through the brick-street section of town, where yard after yard is blanketed with brightly colored blossoms.

There is a large garden at an intersection of two streets that seems to be the unofficial center of the trail. Its two-acre

lot slopes gently down and back up, displaying a huge array
of mature azaleas. Tall pines offer shade, and the small dogwood trees bend gracefully underneath. This garden and
the ones nearby attract thousands of sightseers every year,
and for two weeks a traffic jam of cars and pedestrians clog
these usually quiet side streets.

As I was driving by last February, something nudged
me to stop and look at this familiar place in its solitude,
before the blooms burst out and people crowded its side-
walks. I parked, climbed out of my van, and walked up
to the low stone fence that kept onlookers from wandering
into the garden. I could see the azalea buds, but no color. I
pulled down a dogwood tree branch and inspected its tight,
woody buds that would soon unfold into white four-petaled
symbols of the cross (as the legend goes), with "wounds" at
the tip of each petal.

A squirrel sat on a branch just above, glaring at me. It
barked incessantly, as if to say, "Come back when we're
open! The show doesn't start for another month!" But I had
come before the "show" on purpose. I wanted to see this
place, to hear what messages it could speak even before the
curtain rose on its two-week run of glory.

Way back into the garden, almost out of sight, I saw
a camellia still in bloom. I had never known there was
a camellia bush amid the azaleas, because the camellias
bloom in January and February. Most of us come only in
March or April.

As I opened myself to the silence of the garden, I began
to realize how much was happening there. The soft azalea
buds had been in the making for months, and now color was
just about to peek out. The dogwood branches were bare,
but inside the wood, life was flowing invisibly to bring these
hard bud casings to the point of breaking open into graceful
blossoms. I began to feel the excitement and beauty of preparation, the hidden activity that was brimming just underneath the surface of this place. Without this unseen activity,
there wouldn't be an Azalea Trail, crowds of admiring

sightseers, or a banner of bright color all over everything.

I will remember that sight, that feeling of quiet anticipation, when I am waiting to experience more of God's compassion—especially if I am in pain. Because sometimes it is February in my soul, and I wonder why everything looks bare.

But in God's enigmatic plan, essential things are going on inside me, just under the surface. These are my days of preparation.

FOREVER AND EVER AND EVER

In her novel *The Secret Garden*, Frances Hodgson Burnett tells the story of a walled garden which has amazing powers to bring healing—of body, soul, and spirit—to the children who discover and tend it. Collin, an eleven-year-old brat who thought he would be deformed, disabled, and die an early death, begins to come to the garden daily, works in it, and finds life and hope inside its walls.

Collin describes this spiritual change as a growing awareness that he "will live forever and ever and ever." One passage from the book is like a "bouquet" picked from the garden of God's compassion.

> One of the strange things about living in the world is that it is only now and then you are quite sure you are going to live forever and ever and ever. You know it sometimes when you get up at the tender solemn dawn-time and go out and stand alone and throw your head far back and look up and up and watch the pale sky slowly changing and flushing and marvelous unknown things happening until the East almost makes you cry out and your heart stand still at the strange unchanging majesty of the rising sun—which has been happening every morning for thousands and thousands and thousands of years. You know it then for a moment or so.

And you know it sometimes when you stand
by yourself in a wood at sunset and the mysterious
deep gold stillness slanting through and under the
branches seems to be saying slowly again and again
something you cannot quite hear, however much
you try. Then sometimes the immense quiet of the
dark blue at night with millions of stars waiting and
watching makes you sure; and sometimes a sound of
far-off music makes it true; and sometimes a look in
someone's eyes.[14]

If we will open our hearts and tune our senses to the
melodies of His compassion, the Father of all comfort will
communicate His tender heart in ways we can hear, see, and
feel. This is the true path to finding life in the pain.

8

Finding Life in the Pain

ઽ

*The angel said to the women, "Do not
be afraid, for I know that you are looking
for Jesus, who was crucified."*
MATTHEW 28:5

W e were driving east on Thirty-fourth Street. Most of
the commercial buildings and signs that streamed
by outside the van window were familiar. Some were new.
Although it had been twenty years since I'd been to the old
Lubbock cemetery, I knew generally how to get there. I
thought I could "feel" my way and give Lloyd directions
as we drove.

Looking out the window, I drew inside myself, thinking
how long the trip back to this place had really been. Not
just the nine-hour drive to Lubbock from Tyler, where
we were stopping on our way to a family vacation in
Colorado, but the twenty-year journey back to this piece of
ground. Since the funeral, I deliberately had never visited
my father's grave.

I remembered a number of times, while I was in college
and living at home, that Mother had invited me to go with
her to the cemetery. Because of my emotional resistance and

my overly intellectual spirituality, I shrugged off her offers, saying that I didn't want to go because Dad wasn't there anyway. Why visit a plot of grass?

I know now the reason for my refusals. That plot of grass was a reminder of the pain, and I didn't want to be reminded of grief *or* of the fact that I was as callous as the marble headstone that bore my father's name. Hadn't he caused us enough grief? Why would I want to visit a grave—least of all with my mother? Why make it harder on both of us?

FINDING THE ROAD BACK THROUGH THE PAIN

As we reached the part of town where I thought the left turn to the cemetery should appear, it was gone. In its place were divided highways and an overpass, and even though I could see where the cemetery was, I couldn't see how to get there. There were no signs, and the only way off Thirty-fourth Street led to this overpass. The "old way" wasn't going to get me to the cemetery, and I didn't know the new way.

That's when Lloyd's natural sense of direction took over.

"Oh, yeah," he said. "It's this way." He turned onto the overpass, continued for a quarter of a mile to an exit ramp, and we were there.

Later, as I was writing in my journal, it dawned on me that even finding the *physical* path back to my father's grave had been difficult, just like my *emotional* journey back to his memory. The "old way" wasn't going to get me there, and I needed help to find the new way.

Watching the Road Signs

The first year I went to a counselor, she naturally probed into my relationship with my father. One day when I was wrestling with my frustrations over Lloyd's busy schedule and why it was so hard for me to accept, she said, "I wonder if there's a parallel between Lloyd's occasionally not coming home at night, or during on-call weekends, with your dad's absences because of his drinking binges."

Before a thought-response could even enter my head, my eyes filled and my throat knotted. I don't remember what I said, but I remember being unable to stop the tears. It was my first realization that I was responding to Lloyd from the same emotional place inside that I had once responded to my dad. I had locked up a room inside me and thrown away the key. Now something was turning a new key in the lock.

What also became clear was that I was keeping my husband at an emotional distance out of fear. I was renewing an old habit, formed when I had learned to lock my dad out of my heart. In my complaints about Lloyd's emotional inaccessibility, I became aware that I, too, was holding him at arm's length. Not because he deserved to be feared, but because I was afraid to trust him. I was protecting myself.

During this time, Lloyd and I started spending Wednesday afternoons together. As I recognized that he was *not* my dad and consciously chose to trust his love, I gradually began to open my heart to him and pour out my thoughts and feelings about anything and everything. And he listened. I learned not to expect a certain response from him. I knew he could be trusted, even if he didn't always say, think, or feel exactly what I would have liked. He was being himself, and I was learning to do the same. He also felt free to talk, but his need wasn't as great as mine. And I grew to accept that, too.

As he did with the physical road, Lloyd has helped me find the emotional road back to the memories of my dad. When I struggle in our marriage relationship, it sometimes taps an emotional pattern that reconnects me with the pain over my father. The early problems with Lloyd were like road signs that led me back to a deeper healing of an old wound.

Healing is what brought me to Lubbock on that sunny July morning. Even though it would delay our trip, Lloyd had been willing to spend a half-day in my hometown to let me take time at Dad's grave. So that morning, we checked out of our motel, finished breakfast by eight o'clock, and started to the cemetery. But I had one more stop to make along the way.

We pulled into an old grocery store near the cemetery. The night before I had thought of taking flowers to the grave, but that tradition just didn't seem to fit. I wouldn't bring my dad flowers if I were coming to visit him, I thought. And that's what I planned to do: visit him. Then I remembered something from childhood.

Sometimes on summer evenings, Dad would come home from work with two grocery sacks full of fruit, and that would be dinner. I loved it! Along with the grapes, bananas, apples, plums, and peaches, I enjoyed the delicious novelty and spontaneity of the event. No one had to cook or do dishes. It was a picnic on Dad!

That's it! I thought. *I'll take fruit.* It was good just to be doing something I knew he'd like, something different. It felt almost daring. Novelty and spontaneity—those were things my dad, despite his problems, had brought into our lives. They were parts of me that I wanted to reclaim.

Looking for the Legacy
When we followed the map they gave us at the cemetery office, we soon found the spot. A line of elm trees by the road offered plenty of shade where we parked, let Brian down on his lift, and walked to the grave site.

In this semi-arid climate, nights and mornings are cool and refreshing. This morning was especially so. The ceaseless West Texas breeze brushed against my skin like a familiar caress. I breathed the scent of the newly mown grass.

As I read the map, I saw that the "street signs" in the cemetery were all named for flowers or blossoming plants. Funny thing—until now, I'd never thought of a cemetery as a kind of garden. But it is a place where we dig, plant mere shells that hold true life, and water them with our tears. Those who plant with faith in Jesus (who was once mistaken for a gardener), plant in hope and assurance.

We all stood near the small, flat stone. Since Brian and Mark knew so little, I wanted to tell them about the grandfather they never knew. For about five minutes I described his life as I knew it: he was a good car salesman, he liked to play golf, he had a beautiful, mellow tenor voice and sang solos at church when I was young. I told them of his charm and sense of humor—how on the many nights he was there for dinner, he would tell us the latest joke he had heard that day.

That's the legacy of my father, according to what he did and liked. I never really knew who he was. I also told the boys he had a problem: he drank alcohol too much.

I decided not to tell them how he died, and they didn't ask. *At eight and six*, I thought, *they're not quite ready*.

Mark had been dueling a nearby cedar tree with a stick, appearing not to listen. But before they left to drive a little way off (where they could play, I could have privacy, and Lloyd could be near for my peace of mind), Mark picked a yellow dandelion and said, "Here, Mommy. This is for you."

I hugged him and thanked him. Then I laid the wild flower on the small, gray marble gravestone, right beside the apple, peach, grapes, and plum.

৯

I hadn't expected to learn any family history just from being at Dad's grave. But I did.

His mother's stone and the date of her death told me that my father was seventeen when she died of some disease. (I had thought he was twelve or thirteen.) I wondered how she felt leaving two sons still at home. Since Dad's father left soon after her death, I realized that this seventeen-year-old had lost both parents at the same time. That helps explain why he dropped out of high school.

The stone beside my dad's told another story I had almost forgotten, having heard it only once. There was a member of the family who died in childhood. According to the dates, when my dad was six, his three-year-old brother Ben died. At the age Mark is now, my father lost a brother he had played with and probably helped care for. Because his own father was also an alcoholic and a rather stern man, I doubt he was able to model healthy grieving. At such a tender age, my dad probably never finished mourning the loss of his little brother.

Then I remembered the stone that wasn't there. An older brother, Harper, died when he was a young adult. Although I heard very little of the story, what crept between the lines and innuendos was that Harper left home and lived a life of dissipation.

When I fit the pieces together, I realized that by the time Dad was eighteen, he had lost three members of his immediate family prematurely. He never talked about any of them. I never had any sign that Dad had grieved, only that he had learned how to cover up the pain.

I had come to the grave to talk about *my* pain and loss—to bridge the gap between us. In an unexpected way, by being there with him, I had let him tell me a little more about *his*.

STEWARDS OF OUR PAIN

One of the important things I realized early in counseling was that when I buried grief and anger, I wasn't gaining control of them: I was *giving up* control. They were burrowing somewhere deep inside my heart and poisoning the roots of my soul, which resulted in half-hearted relationships, or overly-intense ones, angry eruptions over little things, and a quiet melancholy that was baffling.

It wasn't until I began to take seriously the stewardship of my emotions that things began to change—ever so slightly. I'm no overnight wonder, to be sure, because I still have bouts with the symptoms of emotional cover-up. But I am experiencing the benefits of being a steward of my pain—facing, feeling, and focusing the God-given energy of my emotions in order to let them serve His purposes in my life. Otherwise, the energy recycles as just another source of silent pain. Having God's compassion for myself—a loving acceptance of my negative feelings, without getting stuck in them—has helped me feel more emotionally alive.

When our nine-year-old friend Catie died of leukemia, we attended the memorial service as a family. For the first time, I was able to weep freely in public. I no longer feared being overwhelmed by grief, or being judged weak in faith. As I wept softly, I heard Brian whisper, "Dad!" He grabbed Lloyd's arm and asked worriedly, "Why is Mom crying?"

I knew that it was okay for me to cry, and that Brian would be okay, too. And I wasn't so loud that I was embarrassing him by making a scene. Trusting Brian's heart to God, I didn't let his distress dry my tears.

Because we had come in separate cars, after the service Brian and I drove home together. On the way, something happened that made us both laugh out loud. Brian quickly asked, "Mom, are you all right? Are you not sad anymore?"

"You know, sweetie," I paused and smiled into the rear view mirror, "sometimes if you cry when you're sad, then you're more able to laugh when you're happy."

I was feeling the goodness of being able to mourn when it's time to mourn and laugh when it's time to laugh. It was the goodness of being able to feel my emotions honestly and work through them. I recalled how feeling anger over Catie's death had helped me express my anger at the Lord over Brian's suffering, and find His healing, accepting compassion. When I had been angry at God in the past, sometimes I took it out on Brian, Mark, or Lloyd, and I regret having been so slow to learn. But the Lord was waiting patiently with His compassion—waiting for me to believe it enough to pour out my heart to Him.

Finally, in desperation, I cried out until my eyes were opened. Frederick Buechner writes,

It is not that God has to be pestered into compassion by our persistence, but that it is only through persistence, through hoping against hope, believing despite doubt, that a man can open himself to receive the compassion that is there in abundance. It is only when you ask a question out of your very bowels that the answer is really an answer. It is only when you stretch out your hands for it until your arms ache that a gift is really a gift.[1]

I felt that I had asked "out of my very bowels," and the Lord had answered out of His *splangchna*, His deep yearning to show compassion.

Coaxing Feelings Out of Hiding

Over the years, something that has concerned me about Brian is his reluctance to express his feelings about disability or death. He can cry at the drop of a hat when Grandma or cousins leave town after a visit, or when he's disappointed. But when the subject of death or his disability come up, he disconnects completely, and quickly changes the subject.

So, typically for him, he hadn't shown any emotion over Catie's death in those days before the memorial service, even though she had been in his Sunday school class and our families are good friends. But there was nothing I could do.

That day as we drove home from the service, right after I had talked about sadness and joy, he finally broke his silence.

"Well, you know what I'm mad about?" he blurted in an angry, quivering voice. "I'm mad that someone has to die when they're only nine years old!"

"Yes," I answered. I wanted to stop the van, get on my knees beside his wheelchair and hold him in my arms, but we were stuck at a stoplight. By the time we were moving again, he had flopped right back out of his feelings. He had said all he wanted to say, and the door to his heart was shut again. But it had swung open for a moment. Maybe it was because he had seen that you can have those scary feelings and still find your way back.

In the Garden Alone

That day at the cemetery, after learning more about my father's pain from the silent stones, I was sitting quietly, listening to the birds sing and the wind blow through the trees.

The words of a song came to mind. It was one I remembered my dad singing at church when I was young. Sometimes, in the early hours on Sunday morning, he would be practicing a solo in the living room, and his voice would awaken me.

> I come to the garden alone,
> While the dew is still on the roses;
> And the voice I hear, falling on my ear,
> The Son of God discloses.
> And He walks with me, and He talks with me,
> And He tells me I am His own.[2]

I had come here to talk to my dad. But I knew it would feel strange to talk to a grave. Now, the words to this old hymn helped me sense the Lord's presence and realize that I could talk to my dad as if I were talking to the Lord. I prayed that His Spirit would guide and protect me, and that my talking "into the air" wouldn't be silly, because I felt odd about doing something so mystical.

Then, though my voice sounded hollow, I began.

"Dad, I came here to talk to you, but it's hard because we were never able to really talk. Somehow, I want to get closer to you now. I'm sorry I locked you out of my heart even after I became an adult. I did it to protect myself from the pain of your drinking, your neglect, and the awful distance between us. I'm sorry I didn't know how to feel compassion for you—to be a daughter to you—when you had emphysema and lived alone. I was afraid of you and of the pain. But I don't want to lock you out anymore.

"I don't know where to start. . . .

"I do wish you could have known Lloyd and Brian and Mark. You would have liked them. You could have taken Mark to play golf and Brian to baseball games. In fact, Brian is a lot like you—friendly, talkative, loves to sing and tell jokes. You two would have really hit it off."

With that, the first tears stung my eyes, and it felt like a rusty door of my heart was starting to open. I felt both fear and joy when I realized how much Dad and Brian were alike. But I chose the joy. By grace, Brian can realize the potential of all Dad's good qualities, despite his handicap. At the age of nine, in some ways he already has.

"Dad, I need to tell you how I felt when you would come home in the night drunk and fight with Mom. I was sad and scared. When you would slam the door and leave, I was afraid you'd never come back, and in my earliest years, I was almost hysterical with grief. As I grew older, somewhere deep inside, I became angry at you, *so angry* at you. But I didn't admit it, because I had to be a good girl. I just felt nothing."

Tears choked out my words again. . . .

ॐ

My thoughts drifted back to a dream I'd had during the early months of counseling.

Dreams are fascinating. In the Bible they were often significant events or channels of God's communication. Sometimes dreams can be helpful in understanding our own inner turmoil or growth. I have paid attention to only a handful of my dreams, but one unusual one had the startling effect of resurrecting my emotional connection to my dad.

During this time period I had been thinking about his influence on our home and my responses, but I hadn't been able to feel any anger at him. I had so closed him out of my life that I could talk about him without blinking an eye.

I could tell you how he had abused or neglected us, but I never felt a lump in my throat or a clenched jaw when I spoke.

It was tempting to believe (as I had believed for years) that my willful, mental forgiveness of him had done the job of delivering me from anger. But my emotional struggles with Lloyd (and with God) were telling me otherwise. I was keeping Lloyd emotionally at bay. And God, though administratively loving, was still sitting in that easy chair across the room. I had never been able to express anger toward either of them without feeling extreme guilt or fear.

In this dream, I was in the large living room of a strange house where a party was going on. Some of the people were familiar, some were relatives, some were strangers. I was lying on a double bed at one side of this large room and soon my dad was there, too. When he climbed on top of me, I felt enraged.

"Get off!" I screamed. "You don't have any right to do this! *You don't have any right!*" I fought him with all my strength. No one in the room noticed or responded to my cries. That's when I woke up trembling with rage.

I have no memories of my dad sexually abusing me, and I don't think this dream means that it happened. What the dream did for me was open up the anger at my dad that had been locked inside my heart for so long. For the first time, it allowed me to feel my rage at him over his emotional abuse and abandonment of the family—of me, my mother, and my siblings.

As I talked through it with Lloyd the next evening, I pounded the coffee table and gave angry words to my once-silent anguish over my father's actions. Lloyd listened, accepted my rage, and voiced his sorrow over my pain and loss. There was nothing he could do except let me cry on his shoulder. That was all I needed.

For the first time, I had stood up for myself without guilt and knew that my father had no right to do what he did, even though he was a victim, too. It was the first time

I knew I didn't have to just say, "Well, that's okay. I forgive you." That passive, easy forgiveness had been a refusal to feel the pain of anger and an obstruction to true intimacy and reconciliation.

Deep, heartfelt forgiveness became possible for me only after I'd felt the pain, because it meant I was finally willing to renew emotional contact with the one who hurt me. Only the Lord could work forgiveness in the depths of my emotional heart, and I would have to wait for Him, as I was willing both to hurt and to love.

That's what the cross was about: the place where Jesus hurt because He loved. I don't pay the penalty for sin, as He did, but I need to be willing to feel the pain, as well as the joy, before I can relate in Christlike love with fallen people. Just as they feel pain, in addition to joy, over relating to me.

Where Were You?
The song continued in my head. *Why did I remember it so well after so long?*

> He speaks, and the sound of His voice
> Is so sweet the birds hush their singing,
> And the melody that He gave to me
> Within my heart is ringing.

"Lord, why is such a sweet song fastened in my heart to my dad?" I spoke now to my heavenly Father. "I was dying inside because he wasn't there. Those dark nights full of pain, I desperately wanted him to come hold me and tell me everything would be okay."

The next part of my conversation I later distilled into a poem, as a way of gathering the pieces of my broken heart.

> Where were you, Daddy, all those dark nights
> when you never came home?
> Where were you when a man

who looked like you came stumbling
through our room in the darkness,
but smelled like all the shame
I remember?

Where were you when I needed
your arms around me
and you goosed my knee instead?
Where were you when I needed
a man's love and there was no one
I could trust?

Where did you go when you fought with Mom
at midnight, slammed the door
and disappeared into darkness?

Where were you when you sang
of Jesus in the garden and Jerusalem's gates,
when I hoped you were there
and would help me find the way?

Where were you when you lost your dad
to drink and your mom to disease?
Where were your yesterdays, your hopes
and dreams? Where was your home
when no one wanted you?

Where were you, Dad,
when you wrote the note
and said we would "gather at the river"?
Where were you when I needed
your life
and you gave it away?

Where are you, Dad?
How can I touch you now?

When will you hold me close
and sing only to me? . . .

Please don't slam the door
on my darkness again . . .
and this time,
this time
I won't slam the door
of my heart on you.

My rage—so connected with my tears—had finally opened
the door to the big, dark room in the mansion of my soul.
It had awakened my heart to feel the tenderness and the
desire, as well as the pain. The sweet song that the Lord
was singing was the bittersweetness of opening my heart
to my dad again, of wanting him to sing only to me.

There is still some grief—missing Dad, and missing
what he might have been. But with it comes a softer heart,
a willingness to trust again because I know I can do more
than just survive. The pain won't kill me, as I must have
thought as a child. In a sense, I had "stood up" to my dad,
refusing to be a victim by repressing my anger and, with it,
my love. But I could also stand *beside* him, refusing to be an
offender by giving up my compassion and my connection
to him—and in the process giving up part of myself.

THE MELODY THAT HE GAVE TO ME

"Even though you brought pain, Dad, you also brought joy.
Thank you for bringing liveliness into our family with your
laughter and singing. When things were good, you made
our lives richer.

"I already have your love of music. Of course, Nan and
Laurie carry your gift into this generation, but I have a
soul-deep appreciation for song because of you. It's as if
through music, you planted in me a desire for intimacy with
God—the walking, talking, tells-me-I-am-His-own kind of

love for the Lord that I enjoy in some measure today.

"Through your music and Mom's prayers, the two of you really have led us spiritually. You planted a vision in my heart—a vision not of the eyes but of the emotions, of the soul that pants after God. You were a person of deep feeling, too, weren't you, Dad?

"When you left the note, and said we would gather at the river, you had faith that God would take you to heaven. It was a message of hope to all of us, wasn't it? He who is forgiven much, loves much, Jesus seemed to say. Dad, you and I have both been forgiven much.

"I look forward to seeing you again in heaven, because then you'll be healed and *truly* happy. It will be a joy to see you as you really are.

> I'd stay in the garden with Him
> Though the night around me be falling,
> But He bids me go; through the voice of woe,
> His voice to me is calling.
> And He walks with me, and He talks with me,
> And He tells me I am His own.

"I have to go now, Dad. I probably won't come back here, though. Our connection isn't here, really. If I could, I would ask you for a hug, but I'll ask Lloyd and the boys instead.

"Until we gather at the river. . . ."

These final words brought different tears for me. Tears of healing, tears of hope, tears of loving enough to miss someone.

❧

It's hard to identify the fruits of something as subjective as this kind of reconciliation. And it probably isn't important to know exactly. But I do think some things have changed since that July day.

The very next week during family camp, I felt more

lighthearted and uninhibited. I plunged into costumes, skits, and singing with uncharacteristic fervor. On the last night, the camp leaders gave numerous awards for almost everything. And although my good friends would find it hard to believe, I proudly carried home a three-inch trophy for "Most Enthusiastic Camper!"

Another change I've noticed is that I'm more comfortable trusting Lloyd, even if I'm disappointed. I'm less afraid to express my anger responsibly to him, and I'm not as afraid of his anger. I have felt more at ease with my sexuality, a little more comfortable with intimacy. Lloyd tells me that I seem more affectionate and responsive. Of course, I still exasperate him with my oversensitivity sometimes, but we're learning to weather those storms better, too.

A few months ago I noticed something else. For years I had had recurring dreams once or twice a month of a faceless man (not always the same one, but someone I didn't recognize) who would chase me, or try to break in, or threaten me with violence. I would cry out, wake up suddenly, and my body would tremble for twenty or thirty seconds. I thought everybody had these kinds of nightmares regularly.

Then, last spring I realized these dreams were disappearing. In the past year, I've had only one or two. I can only guess, but the change in dream patterns may mean that I'm less fearful of men.

I know that my dad isn't as faceless as he once was. And that even though I still bear the scars of our old wounds with each other—and sometimes they still ache—he can't wound me now.

Because I don't hate him anymore.

THE TOMB OF OUR PAIN

Because of her past, Mary Magdalene was no stranger to sorrow, so it didn't bother her to go with the women to the garden tomb where Jesus had been placed. There were the spices to apply, and there would be time to weep with her friends, something she needed very much. But when they arrived, everything changed.

The stone was moved.

The body was gone.

What had happened?

The disciples came in a flurry and then left.

But Mary stayed. She wept in confusion and pain. Then she bent down to look in the tomb again. Angels appeared.

"Woman, why are you crying?" the two voices asked.

"They have taken my Lord away," she said, "and I don't know where they have put him."

Then, from behind her, a single voice echoed, "Woman, why are you crying?"

She glanced back over her shoulder, saw it was the gardener, and bowed her head again to weep.

"Mary," the voice said.

This time she whirled around, because she knew it was Jesus as soon as He spoke her name.

"Teacher!" she cried and ran to Him.

ã

I learn from Mary that if we're willing to go to the tomb of our pain and confusion—to desire openness and honesty even when it hurts—we'll find Jesus there . . . *alive*. Even though all the details of His plan have not yet been completed, He will be truly there, intimately calling us by name, giving us the precious gift of Himself:

> Christ never promises peace in the sense of no more
> struggle and suffering. Instead, he helps us to
> struggle and suffer as he did, in love, for one another.
> Christ does not give us security. . . . Instead, he tells
> us that there is nothing in this world that is forever,
> all flesh is grass. He does not promise us unlonely
> lives. His own life speaks loud of how, in a world
> where there is little love, love is always lonely. Instead

of all these, the answer that he gives, I think, is himself. If we go to him for anything else, he may send
us away empty or he may not. But if we go to him for
himself, I believe that we go away always with the
deepest of all our hungers filled.[3]

And that's all that will matter.

At the tomb of my pain, I had found the Lord alive. Not
visible, as Mary had found Him; but alive within my own
heart, as He turned a grave into a garden of new life. He
brought His light and warmth back into that dark, closed
room of my soul where I had hidden all my feelings toward
my father. The only reason I could have entered that darkness was that Jesus had shown me His compassion for my
own grief and anger.

The pain is not all gone, and my sin is not all gone.
But the pain isn't bitter, and my heart is more tender and
compassionate, because I have experienced Jesus' healing
compassion for me.

Somewhere deep down inside, He takes me in His
arms.

He tells me I am His own.

And I hear Him singing . . . only to me.

PART THREE

HELPING

9

Building a Compassionate Community

ै

My cup overflows.
PSALM 23:5

ें

You will be like a well-watered garden.
ISAIAH 58:11

As we desire to share the compassion of Jesus Christ with others, we need to begin by asking if we are full of God's compassion for ourselves: full and overflowing.

When we know and have felt God's compassion for us, then that sympathy and comfort spills over into the lives of others. Paul says it best:

> Praise be to the God and Father of our Lord Jesus Christ, the Father of compassion and the God of all comfort, who comforts us in all our troubles, so that we can comfort those in any trouble *with the comfort we ourselves have received from God.* For just as the sufferings of Christ flow over into our lives, so also through Christ our comfort overflows. (2 Corinthians 1:3-5; emphasis added)

Until the last few years, I had no comfort to offer other women in silent pain. I went through the motions and tried

207

to be supportive, but I was frozen inside. I was afraid of my pain . . . and theirs.

BECOMING A GARDEN

Rather than leading others to the garden of God's compassion as if it were some far-off place, we can actually bring the garden to them. By Christ's life in us, *our own hearts become His garden of compassion,* and others will enjoy the sympathy and solace they find in our presence.

As we share life in our church, with our friends, and in our families, Christ's compassion—not perfectly, but truly—takes on a richer, deeper reality in our relationships to those around us. For other women in silent pain, we become a living hope that God is present in their pain and that His healing will come.

Wait with Me

Sue Monk Kidd writes that during her struggle through the mid-life years, she learned that a key to inner growth was to "be still" at the deepest places in her heart and let the Lord do His transforming work.

She tells the story of the time a bird flew into the patio door of her home and fell to the ground. She and her two children rushed outside, expecting the bird to be dead, but instead found her stunned, with one wing slightly bruised and lopsided. Sitting perfectly still, the bird allowed her new friends to stroke her gently. After a while, the children went back inside, but Sue stayed with the wounded bird.

> I sat beside her, unable to resist the feeling that we shared something, the two of us. The wounds and brokenness of life. Crumpled wings. A collision with something harsh and real. I felt like crying for her. For myself. For every broken thing in the world.
>
> That moment taught me that while the postures

of stillness . . . are frequently an individual experience, we also need to share our stillness. The bird
taught me anew that we're all in this together, that
we need to sit in one another's stillness and take up
corporate postures of prayer. How wonderful it is
when we can be honest and free enough to say to one
another, "I need you to wait with me," or, "Would
you like me to wait with you?" . . .

I studied the bird, deeply impressed that she
seemed to know instinctively that in stillness is
healing.[1]

This tender story quietly spoke to me of the value of
simply *being with one another* in our hour of need. One of my
favorite names for God in the Bible is Immanuel, "God with
us." Jesus was born a man to be *with us* in our humanity.
He continues to *live within us*—when we trust in Him as
our only Savior. Most startling of all, He *changes us inside*
by living within us in His resurrection power. And although
we cannot change one another, we can wait with each other
in the stillness, with the privilege of seeing God's healing
power at work.

HANNAH: A MODEL FOR WOMEN IN SILENT PAIN

In the context of the church, I would love to see the Lord
magnify His compassion by making groups similar to those
I have attended available to more Christian women (and
searching nonChristians). These groups create an environment that allows women to wait in the stillness with each
other as the Lord heals their "bruised wings" of silent pain.
Whether because of unresolved issues from the past or
confusing stages of growth in the present, they need a place
to be still. Mature Christian women who are sensitive to
the Lord's leading could offer this kind of refuge for those
who desire it.

Although many churches have these kinds of small

groups, some church leaders may be hesitant to authorize them, perhaps because of misunderstanding and fears that such a ministry is potentially "uncontrollable." Nevertheless, many women in silent pain want spiritual leaders to recognize their needs, but they don't know how to begin to articulate them.

One woman in the Old Testament has become a model for me of handling her silent pain in the community of faith. And her spiritual leader, while at first confused and doubtful, may be a model for the church, as well.

Drunk with Sorrow

Hannah was a woman in silent pain. She couldn't have children, which was as big a stigma then as not having a "real job" is today. (Actually, it was much worse.) Most of the time, Hannah's pain lurked within her like a low-grade fever: she felt it, but she didn't pay much attention to it— until "that time of year" triggered a rise in her temperature.

Every year Elkanah's family traveled to Shiloh to sacrifice to the Lord. What should have been a festive occasion turned sour when the antagonist in this little drama appeared: Peninnah, Elkanah's other wife, who had children and wouldn't let Hannah forget it. Every time they headed for Shiloh, like an irritating alarm clock, piercing Peninnah would reawaken Hannah's silent pain, "provoking her in order to irritate her" (1 Samuel 1:6):

> This went on year after year. Whenever Hannah went
> up to the house of the Lord, her rival provoked her
> till she wept and would not eat. Elkanah her husband
> would say to her, "Hannah, why are you weeping?
> Why don't you eat? Why are you downhearted?"
> (1 Samuel 1:7-8)

Year after year. We can be sure that the passage of time had given Hannah ample opportunity to memorize verses and believe that God would work her trial together for good.

Most likely she had turned her focus to serving others and worked on positive mental habits so that she wouldn't dwell on her problem all the time.

But it usually happens with silent pain that something or someone inevitably rubs against an old wound and reminds us that we've been trying to cover up a hurt buried deep in our soul. Just when we think we've learned to cope, something pops the lid off.

No One to Talk To

Hannah had the same struggle you and I have with silent pain: she ran out of people to talk to. For the first two years, Elkanah may have sympathized with his beloved and let her cry on his shoulder. But after years of sympathy, he'd had enough. So, her grief still unresolved, Hannah had retreated into silence.

When I look back at the false messages that influence us to choose silent pain, I realize Hannah heard them all.

Expressing negative feelings isn't rational, because reason should dominate emotion. When Elkanah asked, "Why are you weeping? Why don't you eat?" he wasn't really expecting any new information after all those years. What he meant was, "You don't have a good reason to still be crying about this." Many men, especially, have difficulty with things that they can't explain logically or figure out how to "fix."

Logically, Hannah knew her tears weren't going to change anything. They were only making everyone miserable (with the notable exception of Peninnah).

Expressing negative feelings is not practical, because emotion disrupts our functioning. Some people encourage others to ignore silent pain by focusing on the practical benefits in the middle of the trial. Hannah did have two practical blessings she could be thankful for. Elkanah truly loved her, rather than Peninnah, and he gave her a double portion of food at the yearly feast. Hannah was loved and amply provided for, so her grief seemed like an impractical disruption in her life.

However, even though both of Hannah's blessings were good reasons to be thankful—as are all God's gifts—they didn't heal the pain of her loss. Being thankful is a command, not a cure-all.

Expressing negative emotion is not loving, because it disrupts relationships. Elkanah pulled out the stopper in response to Hannah's expression of grief. "Don't I mean more to you than ten sons?" he pleaded with her, with true pain in his own heart. He loved Hannah, he had given her everything—and yet here she was still weeping over a loss she faced years ago. He took it personally.

Sometimes, sharing our silent pain with our loved ones triggers a response in them of impatience, or of hurt that we can't find contentment with them. We need somewhere else to go.

Expressing negative feelings is not spiritual, because faith should dominate emotion. Although she was depressed, Hannah went to the feast with her family. But this trip would be different, because she didn't keep her grief bottled up. At first that created problems for her—not only with her husband, but also with the response of those in her community:

> Once when they had finished eating and drinking in Shiloh, Hannah stood up. Now Eli the priest was sitting on a chair by the doorpost of the LORD's temple. *In bitterness of soul* Hannah wept much and prayed to the LORD . . .
> As she kept on praying to the LORD, Eli observed her mouth. Hannah was praying in her heart, and her lips were moving but her voice was not heard. Eli thought she was drunk, and said to her, "How long will you keep on getting drunk? Get rid of your wine." (verses 9-14; emphasis added)

Here is where Hannah's faith showed itself: She wept and prayed to the Lord. She had enough trust in God's compassion to take her bitterness of soul right to His door and knock loudly with her pain. Refusing the refuge of anonymity, she even stood up so everyone would see her.

That takes nerve. The last place most of us have the courage to show our deepest pain, sad to say, is in the church, because we fear we'll be misunderstood and judged.

That's what happened to Hannah. Eli completely misunderstood her outpouring of pain. Judging her from a distance, he jumped to conclusions. "This woman is out of control!" (My paraphrase.) "Where is her gentle and quiet spirit?"

Hannah's Response: Finding a Voice

Hannah disregarded the shame in Eli's accusation and answered firmly, "Not so, my lord; I am a woman who is deeply troubled. . . . *I was pouring out my soul to the* LORD. . . . *I have been praying here out of my great anguish and grief*" (verses 15-16; emphasis added).

Hannah's example encourages us not to let the misunderstanding of our religious communities shame us back into silence. She provides a godly model for addressing the needs of women in the church who are suffering in silent pain. We can learn how to find a voice to break the silence from observing three important points in her respectful reply to Eli:

1. She denies the charge of being out of control ("drunk").
2. She admits her true feelings ("great anguish and grief").
3. She states clearly that her expression of grief is an expression of her faith in God's compassion ("pouring out my soul to the Lord").

Hannah acted on her intuitive sense that pouring out her bitterness of soul to God—no matter what others thought—was one way to express her trust in His tender, compassionate love. She could have written David's words in Psalm 62:5-8, which seem to equate trust with "pouring out" a troubled heart: "Trust in him at all times, O people; pour out your hearts to him, for God is our refuge."

Sometimes we hear the message that expressing our pain is self-indulgent. But notice the outcome in Hannah's experience: *Because Hannah poured out her heart, she was a part of bringing God's blessing to Israel.* This blessing was, of course, the prophet Samuel: the fruit of Hannah's pain-filled conversation with God.

Like Hannah's, our pain may have a purpose, too. Our inability to get rid of silent pain may be a God-given energy to ask, seek, and knock for something God wants to happen — in us and through us.

Eli's Response: The Blessing of Legitimacy

Despite his initial confusion and false accusations, Eli recovered his priestly presence and publicly spoke a blessing over Hannah: "Go in peace, and may the God of Israel grant you what you have asked of him" (1:17).

I can understand Eli's first response. I sympathize with church leaders who are hesitant to develop personal growth groups in their women's ministries. It's tempting to dismiss what you don't understand. But perhaps Eli can be a model for leaders who want to adjust their response to the "Hannahs" in their midst.

We can learn three important lessons from Eli's response to Hannah's explanation:

1. He didn't feel responsible to get involved with the specific problem. (There's no indication he ever knew what Hannah had asked the Lord.)

2. He wanted Hannah to experience peace — something every woman in silent pain desires.

3. He blessed her private requests of God, trusting the Lord to do His will in and through Hannah's life. Rather than criticizing and controlling, he publicly validated her deep longings. *He gave her the blessing of legitimacy.*

Like Hannah, women in silent pain want acknowledgment of the faithfulness of their search. The formation of spiritual/emotional growth groups, according to the provision of called and qualified women to lead them, is one way to let the Hannahs among us experience the presence of the Lord through the compassionate blessing of His people.

After Hannah got her hearing, she went on her way, joined the feast, and "her face was no longer downcast" (1:18).

This is a happy ending. My hesitation with it is that it sounds like a "quick fix" for silent pain. But the story lasted for years.

My recovery from silent pain has taken several years and involved several different means. I haven't "arrived," but I am no longer "downcast." I find encouragement in Hannah's story not only to pour out my heart with faith in God's compassion, but also to seek ways the church can bless others in silent pain.

One local church in our community is blessing this type of small group. Over two years ago, my friend Linda asked the church board to let her begin a New Hope Recovery Group, using the church facilities for a once-a-week meeting. New Hope, which adopted its name and direction from a group that began at First Evangelical Free Church in Fullerton, California,[2] provides a Christian support group for adult children of alcoholics and dysfunctional families, modeled on the Twelve-Step recovery program.

Having attended from the beginning, I have seen our New Hope group provide help and encouragement for over a hundred Christians.[3]

COMPASSION IN THE CHURCH: SPIRITUAL/EMOTIONAL GROWTH GROUPS

New Hope is only one model. Other kinds of groups offer people support plus information gleaned from psychological testing.[4] The test results offer help to those of us who may feel a need for additional insight into our "inner being." Since one of the hallmarks of dysfunctional behavior is denial, the Lord may use them to open our eyes to inner conflicts we haven't recognized — conflicts that often interfere with spiritual growth.

Benefits

Since I had shared the group experience with only seven others, I wanted to find out how other women had benefited from this kind of group. One woman responded:

> For the first time I felt secure enough to really voice a piece of my heart and to bleed off some of its pain. . . . God's compassion had only been a concept to me. I thought I understood it. But I experienced it there in the understanding touch of a hand, an arm around my shoulder, and even sympathetic tears. Compassion is no longer a concept, but an experience I can feel.

A grandmother wrote:

> With the loving support of the group and an over-whelming awareness of Christ's indwelling presence, I was able to welcome and even embrace drastic spiritual surgery. I experienced His love and compassion as He wrapped me in grace while stripping away some of the false and phony supports I had always clung to. He replaced my shame and hidden agendas with joy and openness.

Another woman said:

> I became more able to accept others as they are, rather than criticizing or trying to change them. . . . God's compassion became real to me because, even though I had known Christ for years, I began to experience *on a feeling level* that God was "on my side."

Some have criticized this type of group for being too negative. One minister who no longer lives in this area even warned my friend Frances against proceeding with the groups she was leading because he had seen people "devastated" by the experience.

Although it's true that receiving feedback from group

members or from test results can be painful, a good group leader can help members welcome the truth about where they need to grow. Confessing our sins within the framework of a supportive community is an entirely biblical concept, even when it leads to painful feelings and broken egos.

Of course, not all groups run smoothly. One group in another city, involving women I knew, ended with disillusionment when two friends exchanged bitter words during a vulnerable time of sharing. Situations like this are painful and regrettable, but they are created by the people involved, not the group structure itself. Nor are they sufficient reason to shun these groups in fear: that would be like closing all churches because there have been divisive church quarrels. In Frances's ten-year history with these groups, there has been only one major offense she knew about, and it was handled with a minimum of disruption.

I had the opportunity to ask Dr. Cecil Osborne, director of Yokefellows, Inc., how he would answer those who wonder if this type of small group could potentially be dangerous. He replied,

> First, something we weren't taught in school is that about eighty percent of the personality is emotion, or feeling, and about twenty percent is that magnificent computer, the brain. . . . It just seems ludicrous to me to think that getting in touch with eighty percent of your personality could be dangerous. . . . The brain, or thinking, is responsible to decide whether the feeling is appropriate or not, whether to act on it or not. . . . But in these groups we deal with how we feel about others, God and ourselves.[5]

ENEMY AND FRIEND
IN THE COMPASSIONATE COMMUNITY

As I've struggled to enjoy and share God's compassion, the Lord has introduced me to two important forces: an enemy of compassion called the "savior syndrome," and a friend of compassion that I call "emotional responsiveness."

The Savior Syndrome—
Enemy of the Compassionate Community

The silent pain of those we love often confounds us, and we feel a desperate need to relieve the pain or fix the problem. But that need can often become an enemy of compassion. These are the times when simply "being with" becomes the most important—and the most difficult—expression of compassion. Henri Nouwen explains,

> Simply being with someone is difficult because it
> asks of us that we share in the other's vulnerability,
> enter with him or her into the experience of weakness
> and powerlessness, become part of uncertainty, and
> give up control and self-determination. And still,
> whenever this happens, new strength and new hope is
> being born.[6]

It's difficult to realize that we don't have answers for loved ones who are hurting—especially if we've been raised with the assumption that the "answers" in Scripture can be applied to complex human problems in a "quick-fix" kind of way.

My earliest collision with this painful reality was at seventeen, when my mother was first hospitalized. That first time, I knew I had no solutions. But the next time it happened, after I became a Christian and had studied Scripture diligently for four years, I thought I had the answers for her. I shared my "wisdom" and prayed, but nothing calmed my anxiety over her continual struggle, and nothing I said or did seemed to make any real difference. Whenever she suffered, I was filled with dread, frustration, and unspoken disillusionment with God. All my knowledge of Scripture seemed useless to help the situation.

Now, fifteen years later, I realize that I had stumbled

onto the first pitfall of the "savior syndrome." I was more interested in "fixing" my mother than in having compassion—the kind of compassion that accepts and loves people where they are, shares in their pain, recognizes its limitations, prays in faith, and trusts God for the outcome. I had wanted to solve the problem in order to avoid my own pain. I didn't want to "become part of uncertainty"—uncertainty about circumstances, about my feelings, or about God. But by trying to "fix" her—even in the name of Christ—I set myself over her. Love, honor, and compassion were lost.

Another pitfall of trying to "fix" others is that it distracts our attention from our own sin and pain. To that same extent, it also distracts us from experiencing God's compassion. It's much easier to try to solve someone else's problem than to face and feel our own. After all, we "see" their problem so much better! While I concentrated on Mom's struggle, rather than facing my own pain and sinful reactions, I gave free rein to deep, unhealthy patterns in my life.

My desperate fear of pain and powerlessness over my mother's suffering should have been a signal to me that something was wrong. But the truth from Scripture in my mind (which was considerable) wasn't enough during that time. I also needed more truth about my inner being, but I didn't trust God's compassion enough to enter those dark places within. That's why five years ago, when I came to my own crossroads, Psalm 51:6 was like a road sign pointing toward inner, personal growth: "Behold, Thou dost desire truth in the innermost being, and in the hidden part Thou wilt make me know wisdom" (NASB).

It was clear that the Lord wanted me to open and let Him heal those dark, abandoned places in my soul, so that His life could fill them. *I had been helpless to have compassion for my mother because I was in such great need of it myself.*

Even as I listen to the Scripture's encouragement to bear one another's burdens and strengthen the weak, I can't forget the first lesson in humility: utter dependence on God alone, desperate trust in Christ as the only Savior. Because when I try—even in the name of love—to be a savior with a little "s," I lose the capacity to have real compassion, "to become part of uncertainty," which requires radical faith that God alone can heal the heart.

Emotional Responsiveness:
Friend of the Compassionate Community

In the midst of this helplessness and radical faith, is there anything we can do? In the face of silent pain or the problems we can't "fix," what does it mean to "wait with" one another?

Pray, certainly. Listen, if they want to talk.

Once we begin to let the Lord tenderize our hearts and make us more comfortable with our own feelings, we'll also become more emotionally responsive to those we love. Romans 12:15, "Rejoice with those who rejoice, and weep with those who weep," urges us to participate with others in their expression of emotion. This shared experience is the friend of the compassionate community.

A few years ago, I asked the Lord to begin restoring my tender heart. Not long afterward, I ran into Laura, a new friend who had lost her four-year-old boy after nearly eighteen months of fighting through his disability and their sorrow. Neil had been severely disabled as the result of an accidental near-drowning when he was two.

Because Laura knew we had been through critical times with Brian, she wanted to talk about Neil and the last few weeks of his life. Ordinarily, I would have found the meeting uncomfortable, because of fear that I couldn't sympathize enough, that I wouldn't share in her pain.

As she talked, I didn't feel anything. Then I remembered to ask for help. "Please soften my heart! Don't let me be afraid of this!" I silently prayed.

Then I sensed an urging, as if His Spirit called from within, "Listen. Stay with her. Feel the pain!"

As Laura described Neil's last hours, her eyes filled with tears. And mine did, too. When she finished, we hugged each other for a few extra moments. Then she said, "But the Lord is healing me. He has taught me so much. I know more about why He gave us Neil."

We parted with smiles. I felt sadness without despair, and I also felt grateful for a softer heart.

A few days later, I received a note from Laura. To my surprise, she said what an encouragement I had been, how she had felt blessed and strengthened. I didn't understand, because I hadn't said anything encouraging to her that day.

Then it dawned on me. Max Lucado calls tears "miniature messengers; on call twenty-four hours a day to substitute for crippled words."[7] The Lord had let my *tears* take His message of compassion to Laura.

ॐ

I think women, especially—because it is one of our feminine strengths—can deepen our capacity to be emotionally responsive to people in pain. For me, it's as if the Lord has brought me back to the question that started this whole journey.

"Lord, how do You feel?"

Now the question is not only about what's happening to me, but about what's happening in the world around me. Now that I have become aware of how deep His compassion runs for me, I am more able to "be with Him" as He bares his heart for a hurting world full of hunger, disease, oppression, and violence.

Sometimes this "being with" can make the work of building compassionate communities seem like the impossible dream. As the Lord makes us more emotionally responsive, what keeps the silent and thunderous pain of a suffering world from overwhelming us? What good is it to feel compassion for things over which we have no control? Will we be motivated to act by compassion, or by guilt and pity? What can we do that will really matter in the world?

10

Compassion as Energy

ze.

*When the compassion of Christ is
interiorized, made personal,
and appropriated to ourselves, the break-
through into caring for others occurs.*[1]
BRENNAN MANNING

When I first read Sue Monk Kidd's story about the
wounded bird, it reminded me of my own similar
experience—similar, except for one thing. Sue's feathered
friend healed and flew away. My story had a different
ending.

I was on my evening walk, and the western sky had
turned from pink to gray by the time I rounded the last
corner. Wanting to get home before dark, I was hurrying
up the hill when my peripheral vision caught sight of a dead
bird on the pavement. I whizzed past, not wanting to look
at it. But that evening, something unreasonably told me to
stop and go back.

As I got closer, I saw that the young sparrow wasn't
dead after all. Her eyes were wide open—unusually wide.
Her little chest was heaving rapidly, and her head seemed
stuck to the street. When I knelt down, she didn't startle,
because she couldn't.

She was dying.

Forgetting about the time, I stayed there on my knees watching something I had never before observed first-hand—something alive facing death. Those little eyes were wild with fear, and I felt a twinge of fear, too. As her breath pounded against the inevitable, my pulse beat faster and my eyes filled with tears. It wasn't long until her body stilled and her eyes closed.

As I walked home in the darkness, I marveled that if I could have such compassion for a common bird, how must the Lord feel, the One who created her? And if He feels that way for an animal, how much more must He feel for us? It was as if He had wanted me to kneel at His side that night and share something He feels many times a day at a much deeper level.

&

"Are not two sparrows sold for a cent? And yet not one of them will fall to the ground apart from your Father. . . . Therefore do not fear; you are of more value than many sparrows" (Matthew 10:29, 31, NASB).

Whenever I used to read these words, I would think of how the Lord *knows* every time a sparrow falls. His sovereignty and omniscience mean that He has control and is totally aware—a perfect accountant, so to speak—of all that happens in His world.

But that evening on my walk, a new dimension of Jesus' words welled up in my heart. For every suffering of any of His creatures, my heavenly Father not only *knows*, but *feels* the sorrow and pain that I felt that night. In Jesus Christ, the God of the universe "took up our infirmities and carried our sorrows" (Isaiah 53:4).

FEELING THE PAIN WE CAN'T HEAL

What about the dying birds of this world, the bruised people who don't mend as we wait in the stillness with them? What about the wounds that don't heal? What if I wait with you in faith, yet "deliverance" in this life never comes? Is there any point in feeling the pain then?

Of all the wounds that seem beyond remedy, the world's gaping wounds of hunger, disease, violence, and physical and spiritual oppression are most obvious. We see the starving African woman and her children on the evening news. We hear that while famine spreads, relief work is stretched too thin. We read that starvation, disease, and simple diarrhea kill off forty thousand children worldwide every day. With all our apparent wealth and technology, our best medicine is like a cold rag on the forehead of a dying cancer patient.

So why bother? Why be tenderhearted with compassion for people who are—like that tiny bird—wide-eyed with fear, chests heaving on the inevitable slide downward into death? As one friend put it, "You can't die on every cross." Why feel compassion about something we can't change?

Painful Blessings

In self-defense, I used to callous myself to the media bombardment of worldwide pain. *If I can't change it,* I reasoned, *then it serves no purpose to feel it.* But I've since changed my mind.

As I've opened my heart to the depth of God's tender sympathy for me, I have felt more compassion for others. There was nothing I could do for the sparrow. But as I wiped the tears from my cheeks, I knew I had felt another level of the depth of God's compassion in His willingness to share pain with us. In that little dying, something had come to life in me. My tears became tears of joy that the Christ in me could be so tender as to weep over a bird, so tender as to grieve over *me* and *every person* in pain.

I can't cure the world. But there are blessings in feeling the pain I can't heal. First among them is that *Jesus Christ's heart of compassion is magnified within me.* Simply feeling true compassion can bless others and glorify God, even if there's nothing we can or are called to do. The twofold definition of compassion is a tender sympathy toward one in distress and a desire to alleviate it. That sympathy is the powerful word *splangchnizomai* used to describe Jesus' deep feelings when He saw someone in misery. Brennan Manning writes,

> The numerous physical healings performed by Jesus to alleviate human suffering are only a hint of the anguish in the heart of God's Son for wounded humanity. His compassion surges from the bowels of His being and operates on a level that escapes human imitation.[2]

As we are willing to let our heart beat with God's, as we ask Him to make us more emotionally responsive even to the things we can't change, *He changes us*. Nothing in our natural self can imitate Christ's compassion. But when He lives in us, then that miracle of feeling can occur. Good works may follow from that change of heart—but before any of them happen, we have glorified God by giving Him our emotional being, hurting over what hurts Him. We have let Him occupy another room in the mansion of our souls.

Within those rooms, we will discover the second blessing of feeling the pain we can't heal: *It is the only energy that can generate acts of compassion that have eternal value and temporal stamina.* Without Christ's heart, we will burn out. If we focus on results or recognition, we will become discouraged when they fall through. Only as we believe that our sympathy and our desire reflect God's presence can we accept our limitations and trust God to be sufficient. Only then can we cheerfully continue even in the face of overwhelming odds.

Feeling the pain not only magnifies the Lord in our hearts, it also provides the energy for service, even in situations that seem hopeless. These experiences remind us that we aren't responsible for the results. We are only responsible to reflect Christ's compassionate heart to a broken world.

STORIES OF SERVICE

In his book *A Distant Grief,* F. Kefa Sempangi tells the story of the Christian church in Uganda under the cruelty of dictator Idi Amin in the early 1970s. Despite life-threatening persecution, Sempangi and other Christians organized orphanages for the many children whose parents were killed by the government's mass executions. Still, only a small percentage of the children could be helped. The others were left in desperate squalor.

> For every child we were able to accept, twenty were turned away. We investigated home situations and spent long hours in prayer, and in the end our decisions seemed arbitrary even to ourselves. *This child, not that one. Life for this one, a living death for that one.* The mothers of these rejected children never understood our position. *There is no room, there is another child more desperate,* these are sayings which make no sense at all to the mother of a suffering child.[3]

One very difficult day, as Sempangi was picking up Florence, a young girl selected for the orphanage, a crowd of children begged to be taken along. Sempangi had to pull them out of his car and watch them fall one at a time from exhaustion as they chased his car, shouting, "Take us! Take us, too!"

Sempangi described his bitterness at the Lord:

> It was then that I felt the deep pain which had been growing in my heart. *Oh, Lord,* I cried silently, *where is your concern for these children? Why am I taking one when there are ten others? Why can't you give me the chance to save them all?*
>
> Feeling desperate and abused, I looked over at Florence. She straightened her cloth wrapper. Since her parents' death she had known nothing but

hardship. Her poverty-stricken guardians had used her as a slave laborer and she had never had enough to eat. Now her face beamed in anticipation.

I stared at Florence and in the deep silence of my frustration I heard the convicting voice of Jesus: "Kefa, you are not the Messiah. You are not in charge of my vineyard. You are only one small worker, and this is the task that I have for you. This is the child I want you to take."

. . . In this brokenness I learned that it was not I who was sufficient but God.[4]

When we feel overwhelmed by the hurts we cannot heal, we learn that it is not we who are sufficient, but God.

৯

That was Dotti Fitchett's lesson as well. How else can you open a house for men and women with AIDS who have no place to go, without feeling overwhelmed?

"When I read in the paper that those dying of AIDS were called 'disposable people,' I *knew* how that felt," Dotti told Lloyd and me when we went to visit HIS House. "I had suffered criminal child abuse, was bounced through foster homes, and even spent time in a mental hospital because I was considered a 'disposable person.' Then I came to the Lord through the Salvation Army and served there for eighteen years in several jobs that really prepared me for this. I worked with street people and managed a home for battered women."

Begun in 1989, HIS House (HIV Information/Education Support Services) has provided support and a home for people suffering with AIDS. Dotti, the founder and executive director, said she started the house because the Lord led her to do so after she was laid off as a hospital chaplain. Lloyd had heard about HIS House from patients he treats as a volunteer at the county AIDS clinic. So we decided to find out more about it.

I asked Dotti how she kept up her energy and motivation for such a draining work. (There are six rooms available, and one is a medically-equipped hospice room for those who are dying.)

"One way is through the name of this place. When I first started, some people teased me about this being 'Dotti's House.' And that scared me; it felt like a knife every time I heard it. Then one night, it was as if the Lord made me realize, 'No. It isn't *my* house. It's *His* house.' Then I thought of the acronym."

When we first walked into this large, fifty-year-old Victorian home in north Tyler, I was shocked at how elegant it seemed inside. The batboard walls had been oiled to a deep, rich color, and there was intricate woodwork throughout the interior. It was modestly furnished, but attractive and comfortable, with an old-style decor that fit the house. Without being consciously aware of it, I must have been expecting a run-down house for "run-down" people. But it was truly charming.

We sat and waited for Dotti as she took Albert, the newest resident, to a car where someone would drive him to the doctor's office. Albert, who looked to be sixty-going-on-ninety, with gray beard and disheveled hair, was obviously disoriented and had to be led out the door. The previous night, Dotti told us, an ambulance from a nearby town had arrived at HIS House and "dumped" Albert on the steps. No one had contacted Dotti. "Albert is probably in the latter stages," she explained when she returned, "because he seems to be suffering dementia. He isn't able to function alone, his family can't take him in, and he has no money."

The bad news is that seventeen people have died in the hospice room at HIS House. But the good news, Dotti said, is that eleven of those either came to know the Lord or came back to Him before their death.

"That's another one of the encouraging things here—to see people face death with a sense of peace and security. We have sat and held their hand and cried with them. But those people know that death is the ultimate healing. It's hardest to watch the others die, those who don't know Jesus."

One encouraging element for Dotti and everyone involved is the weekly support group. This group includes not only residents, but volunteers, former caretakers, family members, and interested individuals from the local community. Some of them are HIV-positive and just need the support.

"It's great when families are brought back together through some of the supportive activities of the ministry," Dotti told us. "Family members are asked when they bring the person in whether they can give volunteer time to the house. Sometimes fathers, for instance, can't come and sit in the same room with their child, but they can fix something around the house and feel like they're a part."

The story Dotti told with the most joy was about Susie, the first mother of children who came to the hospice room of HIS House. Susie was bedridden, deaf, and had a history of personality disorders. Her husband had left her once, then come back just long enough to give her AIDS and leave again. She came to the house after she had blown up her home in despair over finding out she had the disease. She had meant to kill herself, but succeeded only in causing her own deafness.

"We had a blackboard that we wrote on," Dotti explained, "and we shared Scripture with Susie, and we asked her questions about her faith. She gave us answers that assured us she was ready to die, that she knew the Lord and was going to heaven."

The problem was that Susie's two daughters were very hostile toward Dotti when she tried to explain that if their mother was cremated rather than buried (as the social worker had suggested because of cost), it wouldn't matter. That their mother would be with the Lord. But the daughters were intractable. In her rage, one of them threw a book at Dotti.

I wondered what it was that would make this child so angry. Eventually, we discovered that the church they had attended believed that AIDS was strictly a homosexual disease and that Susie must have been bisexual. In the church's mind, that was one of the unforgivable sins. They wouldn't bury Susie because they believed she had lost her salvation.

"These children heard this, and they had no hope," Dotti said. "Now I know what Scripture means when it says 'grieving as those who have no hope.' I saw that in these girls. So, a few days later, we set up an overhead projector with transparencies, sat Susie up in a wheelchair, and we asked her questions about her faith while the girls watched. We let Susie write her answers, we let the girls ask questions, and we just 'talked.'"

Dotti said that the following week the younger daughter went back to their church, and during a testimony time, she told them she didn't care what they did about her mother. She told them that her mother knew the Lord Jesus, and that when she died she was going to be with Him forever.

"In a matter of a few days," Dotti continued, "that church had raised thirty-five hundred dollars for Susie's funeral. We had a service here and a graveside service in their hometown with the congregation. That church changed its mind because of Susie's experience and because of Jennifer, who was able to explain it to them. They changed their minds about AIDS and about Christians being separated from the Lord because of their sin."

To me, the workers at HIS House reflect the heart of Jesus, who stood ready to heal and hold sick strangers whether they knew who He was or not. And they talk about Him here, because this is His House.

૪♦

HIS House has captured my heart, because the Christ who was moved with compassion for Dotti Fitchett now reaches out to others through her.

When Christ fills our hearts with compassion—His compassion for us, as well as for others—then we will begin to want to share that compassion with those who have desperate physical and spiritual needs. Maybe at a place like HIS House, maybe somewhere else. By faith, we can know that He has planted in us a heart's desire to serve in some way. But we need to wait for the desire and direction.

We need to wait for the passion.

Of course, we can wait with our eyes, ears, and hearts open. We can wait, asking the Lord, "How do You feel about this?" But if our hearts long to be His, we can wait with assurance that He will touch us deeply at the place we are called to be.

Some may object that this approach can be an excuse to do nothing: "I don't feel led to answer such-and-such a need." But all of God's principles can be abused if we're not in touch with His heart, with His Spirit deep at our core. And this principle doesn't necessarily mean that I have to wait idly.

෨

When I first heard about Saint Marcus Compassion House, I loved the name. I was glad Emanuel and Tina Ward chose this banner for their ministry to people in need.

Emanuel, a cheerful, soft-spoken, articulate man in his thirties, told me about an experience in his life that planted the seed of Compassion House. Years ago, he had been laid off at one job and hadn't yet found another one. After his old car broke down, he was left without a job, transportation, or a place to live.

"Before that, I thought the only people who got that low were the ones who didn't want to work, who were irresponsible and the cause of their own situation," Emanuel commented. "But there I was, not sure where the next meal was coming from. I found out firsthand what it meant to be needy, to need a lift until I could get back on my feet." And later, he did.

That was the passion that started Compassion House. During the past two years it has offered food, clothing, medical and dental assistance, job counseling, child care, and spiritual encouragement to "those who are in need of a shining light in a dark world." Supported by individuals and churches, run by minimal staff and numerous volunteers, these two little brick houses on Line Street (once the target of police drug-raids) are now homes of hope.

About the time I started writing this book, I began going to Compassion House twice a month. The Lord had put a desire in my heart, but I knew that the little time I gave wasn't much. I was there to fill sacks with food, watch and listen, and find out more about the people whose hearts were given to this work.

One day, I was asked to go to the King's Storehouse to pick up a load of food. I had never heard of the place before. When I got there I found a large warehouse, full of food donated by wholesalers, and staffed by volunteers. When I asked the lady in the office who the director was, she just laughed. "Well, this place was begun by a group of Christians. There's not really a director. We have this saying that whoever volunteers the most this week is in charge. So, I guess that's me."

Always ready with laughter and warm hugs, Tina Ward's spirit fills Compassion House with a joy that's contagious. Tina oversees the interviewing, food and clothes distribution, and volunteer training at the house. On an average day, I've seen her talk to applicants, cry with a troubled mother, give the gospel to a man recently freed from prison, and chat with some older women who "just need the company."

"We're here to love them," she says, smiling broadly, "not just give them food. Others can do that, but we want to get to know them, treat them with respect, and let them know we care about them."

Last week I saw Eugenia, a regular volunteer, help a young woman with three children who was about to go into the hospital. After arrangements were made, Eugenia asked the woman casually if she knew Jesus. I didn't hear her response, but soon they disappeared into another room to pray.

At Compassion House spiritual counseling is available, but not imposed. The only requirement for receiving continued assistance is that a person be actively looking for employment. Emanuel offers help in the search.

I don't know where the Lord will plant my heart. But I treasure the opportunities for "seeing Jesus" at Compassion House, sensing His compassion in the hearts of others, and finding Him in the faces of the men, women, and children who come there in need.

CHEERFULNESS: AN EMOTIONAL GUIDELINE

As I begin to be more emotionally responsive, I see how endless are the needs in my church, community, and world. Then the struggle is in knowing what to do and how much is enough. Besides not neglecting my other responsibilities, what else can help me know the path and the limits of God's leading?

I've heard all kinds of advice on this. But the most convincing for me are Paul's words about giving, whether resources or service: "Each man should give what he has decided in his heart to give, not reluctantly or under compulsion, for God loves a cheerful giver" (2 Corinthians 9:7).

I had never thought about cheerfulness as a way to decide what service or how much time or money I can give in faith. But I think that's what this passage is saying. *Don't do something because you "ought to" or "should." Do what or how much* you've decided in your heart you joyfully *want* to do. To me, giving cheerfully means *waiting for the passion.*

The things we do reluctantly, or because we feel compelled (which can be a kind of legalism), may serve a temporary function. But they have little value in God's sight. God loves cheerful giving from the heart, and He'd rather we wait until we discover His passion within us than to give grudgingly. "Whatever you do, work at it with all your heart," Paul says in Colossians 3:23. The Lord doesn't need our service unless our hearts are in it!

I won't make a blanket statement that we're never called to do anything we don't want to do. But regarding service, I think God's leading is much closer to that than I ever thought before. Cheerfulness is like an internal road sign. When I ask, "Where do You want me to serve?" His answer may be, "Wherever you can do it cheerfully."

Cheerfulness can also be an emotional boundary in showing us *how much* we can give. My friend Kris wrestled with how much time and emotional support she could give to a friend who was struggling with ongoing emotional pain. At one point, she became frustrated over realizing that she felt over-burdened. She was still giving herself, but grudgingly. Eventually, Kris realized she had come to the limits of her heartfelt service. So she talked to her friend, reduced her involvement, and trusted that this might allow the other woman to depend more on the Lord and less on her, or to benefit from another woman's encouragement.

When feeling over-burdened starts replacing our cheerfulness, it may indicate that we have gone beyond the limits of our present ability to give from the heart.

Compassion at the Limits
I realize that I have sometimes continued serving beyond the limits of cheerfulness because of pride. I may think I am more generous or servant-hearted than I truly am. Or I want to *appear* more servant-hearted than I truly am. So I plug on.

Then, if I feel imposed upon, I might be tempted to think I am "suffering for Christ," or "taking up my cross." But it's wood, hay, and stubble! The dilemma is caused by my unwillingness to face the limits of my heartfelt compassion and servanthood. That doesn't mean I have to stay at the present level of my "compassion fitness," but I need to admit where I am before I can increase my cheerful endurance. That increase starts on the inside, as I feel Christ's compassion for me and share His heart for others.

Sometimes I'm reluctant to give or serve because I have so little that I can give cheerfully. But something Jesus said forever changed my mind about that: "And if anyone gives even a cup of cold water to one of these little ones because he is my disciple, I tell you the truth, he will certainly not lose his reward" (Matthew 10:42). A cup of water quenches the thirst of just one person for only a few hours, but Jesus said, "It counts!"

The Lord doesn't care as much about *how* much we give as He does about *why* we give. Is it because others in the church are doing it? Or because we feel guilty if we don't do it? Or because somebody said, Do it first and feel it later? Or because we think that if we do loving deeds we will feel loved, and we want to feel loved?

Jesus wants me to do whatever I do not because I am outwardly imitating Him (which is partially possible in our own efforts), but because I am inwardly becoming like Him, because my emotional responsiveness is "following" Him.

When Paul writes about the gifts of the Spirit, he adds his encouragements about *how* to do each job: if the gift is leadership, it should be carried out "diligently"; if it is showing mercy, it should be done "cheerfully" (Romans 12:8).

I used to wonder about this description, because mercy (like compassion) is usually needed when someone is in pain or in great need of some kind. It's often a sad time. Why would Paul mention cheerfulness?

When I look a few verses ahead, I realize that Paul doesn't intend us to avoid sharing grief, because there he reminds us to weep with those who weep. But sometimes, *after* we have wept with others, we find laughter a pleasant relief. That's one way cheerfulness is part of mercy: it reminds us that we don't have to despair even in the worst of circumstances.

So cheerfulness may also be an indicator of the quality of our compassion—whether we are able to "grieve with" in those situations that take us to our limits, and still not lose hope.

COMPASSION IS NOT PITY

It was important for me to learn not only what compassion *is*, but also what it *isn't*. One of the most important distinctions here is that *compassion is not pity*. The Lord doesn't want us to pity ourselves or others in the condescending sense of that word, as it's sometimes understood today.

Although the word *pity* was used differently a hundred years ago, today it "implies tender or sometimes slightly contemptuous sorrow for one in misery."[5] This definition connotes a lack of respect, which is a key quality of compassion.

Pity also implies a loss of hope. As one friend said, "I think pity leaves God out of the picture." As I thought about the differences between compassion and pity as energy for serving those in need, these contrasts came to mind:

Pity	Compassion
Weakens	Empowers
Aggravates wound or lack	Soothes wound or pain
Despairs	Hopes
Denigrates the person	Believes in the person
Is passive (does nothing)	Is active (even if indirectly, e.g., in prayer)
Burns out	Doesn't give up
Discourages	Gives courage
Indulges negative feelings	Validates negative feelings
Patronizes	Respects
Expects doom	Expects eventual resolution
Says "I feel sorry for you"	Says "I feel with you, and I entrust you to God"
Stands above	Stands beside

Whatever I do in response to Christ's compassion within me—whether toward a friend in silent pain or starving people across the world—I want it to be in the spirit of true compassion. By His life in me, I want to empower, soothe, hope and not despair, believe in, actively help, give courage, respect, feel with, and stand beside rather than above.

Kefa Sempangi of Uganda tells how he learned the difference between compassion and pity from one of his "fellow-workers." A Dutch couple who came to their assistance in the orphanage project were Dr. and Mrs. Hans Rookmaaker. Dr. Rookmaaker had been a professor and friend of Sempangi's while Sempangi attended school in Holland.

But it was "Anky," as Mrs. Rookmaaker was affectionately called, who was the driving force in raising funds for the orphanages. Once, when she wanted pictures of some of the children to help her seek Dutch sponsors, Sempangi sent photos of the children taken in their shabby clothes and miserable housing. Mrs. Rookmaaker wasn't pleased.

> "These pictures are ugly," she wrote. "Please send me
> new pictures when the children have eaten properly
> for several weeks and are dressed in mended clothes.
> We don't want to appeal to human sorrow or pity,
> we want to appeal to what is best in our sponsors.
> We want to remind them that these children in need
> are God's handiwork, that they are His beautiful
> creation."[6]

Countless orphans in ravaged Uganda were given dignity and respect, as well as compassionate aid, because one woman loved them as gifts from God, not as objects of pity.

Just as the emotional gauge of cheerfulness can help me decide what and how much to do, a respectful heart of compassion will keep me from prideful pity toward those in need.

Those reminders helped me recently when I was attracted to an article about Christian women in post-Communist Rumania. The author, Mary Ann Bell, and three other American women had been sent on a three-week mission to help their sisters in Christ start women's ministries and small-group Bible studies. Rumanian women have never had such opportunities before.

As I looked at the photographs, I saw women dressed roughly, heads covered with shawls. They looked just like the villagers in the movie *Fiddler on the Roof*. Rumania, unlike some of the other Eastern Bloc countries, was described as tottering on the edge of its own Dark Ages.

During the harsh, Stalinist-type reign of Nicolae Ceausescu, these women saw their country brutally violated and reduced to "unrelenting ugliness." Their hardship was etched on tired, pale faces.

> We'd been told that most women in Romania work eight hours, stand in lines for food, or worse—find there is no food; then go home to prepare, somehow, something for their families to eat in cold, poorly-lit apartments. . . . [One pastor said,] "Romanian women are treated little better than slaves in the home. Although this is not as bad in Christian homes, this is still a problem."[7]

When I saw the picture of one woman, face in her hands, standing beside a simple wooden cross with names of those who died in the revolution, I wanted to cry with her. I have no idea what they've been through, but these are my sisters in the Lord. I found myself wanting to know more about their pain—their silent pain, as well as the thundering ache of oppression, poverty, and bloody revolution.

I felt glad that Christians from a privileged country had gone there to be with them. These Americans listened to their pain, witnessed their brave endurance, brought words of comfort, and offered guidance in starting small groups where women can share God's Word, hope, and comfort with one another. Perhaps as women they can now begin their climb out of the Dark Ages, where they are still segregated in churches and are only beginning to be recognized as "fellow heirs of the grace of life" (1 Peter 3:7, NASB).

When I think about women in silent pain here in this country, now I will think about these Rumanian women, too. I will think of how low their self-esteem may be, pushed down by long years of oppression and overwork. Then I will be reminded that while compassion feels the pain, it also has hope because of the lordship of Jesus Christ over even the worst of the political systems spawned by this troubled world.

I can believe in these women because Christ dwells in them. He loves and respects them, and He will shepherd them tenderly. There must be strong hearts deep inside those plain, weather-worn bodies—strength that has come not from being valued by those around them, but from finding the God of all comfort to be their only refuge.

As Mary Ann Bell walked into the first meeting, where the church had been waiting an hour for their arrival, she watched these women's expressions:

> Young and old alike were listening eagerly, singing joyfully. They did not seem to notice how late it was. I couldn't even imagine such patience in the States. The mood in that packed church was one of anticipation. This was not a social occasion. They had come to meet their God.[8]

Far from feeling pity for these women, or guilt for having so much while they face poverty and discrimination—I felt encouraged by them. *Look at what they've survived, by God's grace!* I tell myself. *And look at what they have to anticipate as they search for a brighter future, with freedom to reach out to their own people!*

I can pray for them, because they, too, have captured my heart with their humility and faith. And if I could go and be with them, I would. I would love to hear these "Hannahs" of Eastern Europe pouring out their pain-filled hearts to the Lord and yet still singing for joy.

LONGING FOR HIS APPEARING

I am no missions activist. This chapter has been more a reflection of my mind and heart than of my service, because I'm still "in process." I don't think women in silent pain need to feel guilty if their arms don't reach around the world.

The Lord wants you to know *first* that His arms reach all the way around you. From that security, you will grow into cheerful giving, because your cup will feel full and over-flowing. In the meantime, you can "wait with" those you love who are in pain; you can "wait for the passion."

Ultimately, we can wait expectantly for Jesus Christ, who will finally complete His plan of compassion for the earth by destroying the last vestiges of sin, suffering, and silent pain. That's the supreme reward that comes to those who have had the courage to feel their own pain and to become emotionally responsive to the heart-cry of history, the groaning of creation ever since the Fall, and the ache of this world's thundering pain:

Our unimaginable ecstasy when we see Jesus.

At the end of his life, Paul wrote,

Now there is in store for me the crown of righteousness, which the Lord, the righteous Judge, will award to me on that day—and not only to me, but also *to all who have longed for his appearing.* (2 Timothy 4:8; emphasis added)

Who knows what a crown of righteousness is? But I do know the King of Compassion. And for those who read this book and feel the fear that silent pain will never end, you may have the biggest emotional investment in "His appearing." In that "crowning moment," the pain will be *over.*

You will know Christ in a perfect relationship.

And you will be filled with love and adoration for the One who has rescued you from it all, if you have simply trusted in Him.

In the meantime, this same Jesus feels every heartache with you. If you could see Him, He would take your face in His hands, look into your eyes with tenderness, and tell you how much you mean to Him—how valuable and wonderful you are, how much He delights in you. Then, He would fold you in His arms and never let go. Never.

Someday, you will see, hear, and feel all of that.

"And so we will be with the Lord forever. Therefore encourage one another with these words" (1 Thessalonians 4:17-18).

While I do rejoice more than ever in knowing Jesus Christ here and now, I still deeply long to see Him. In this life, we will never be free of every silent pain or every longing. But I wait, with a sure confidence, for the day His compassion will wipe away every tear, every silent pain.

When we live forever in His mansion, the mansions of our soul will finally be free of dark, closed rooms. Our heart will be "like a well-watered garden, like a spring whose waters never fail" (Isaiah 58:11).

Notes

CHAPTER ONE: SILENT PAIN: A LOW-GRADE FEVER
OF THE HEART

1. H. Norman Wright, *Always Daddy's Girl: Understanding Your Father's Impact on Who You Are* (Ventura, CA: Regal Books, 1989), page 164.
2. Linda Schierse Leonard, *The Wounded Woman: Healing the Father-Daughter Relationship* (Boston and London: Shambhala, 1982), page 19.
3. Carol J. Kent, *The Secret Passions of the Christian Woman* (Colorado Springs, CO: NavPress, 1990), page 173.
4. Karen Burton Mains, *The Key to a Loving Heart* (Elgin, IL: David C. Cook, 1979), page 40.
5. Dr. Larry Crabb, *Inside Out* (Colorado Springs, CO: NavPress, 1988).
6. Wright, page 151.
7. Leonard, page 3.

8. John Trent and Gary Smalley, quoted on the back cover of Wright.
9. Wright, pages 33-34.

CHAPTER TWO: WHY THE PAIN WON'T GO AWAY

1. Carol J. Kent, *The Secret Passions of the Christian Woman* (Colorado Springs, CO: NavPress, 1990), page 81.
2. Dan Allender, "Shame: What It Means to Fear Exposure," *IBC Perspective*, vol. 1 (Morrison, CO: Institute of Biblical Counseling, 1985), page 23.
3. Sandra D. Wilson, *Counseling Adult Children of Alcoholics* (Dallas, TX: Word, 1989), page 140.
4. Paul Tournier, *The Gift of Feeling* (Atlanta, GA: John Knox, 1979), page 23.
5. Tournier, page 5.
6. Tournier, page 27.
7. Donald W. McCullough, "Why You Don't Have to Cheer Up," *Christianity Today*, 5 November 1990, page 22.
8. David E. Carlson, *Counseling and Self-Esteem* (Waco, TX: Word, 1988), page 23.
9. Carlson, page 175.

CHAPTER THREE: THE SPECIAL NEEDS OF WOMEN IN PAIN

1. "Depression Strikes Women More," *Tyler Morning Telegraph*, 12 December 1990.
2. Mary Stewart Van Leeuwen, "Life After Eden," *Christianity Today*, 16 July 1990, page 20.
3. Linda Schierse Leonard, *The Wounded Woman: Healing the Father-Daughter Relationship* (Boston and London: Shambhala, 1982), page 120.
4. Leonard, page 121.
5. Leonard, page 121.
6. C. S. Lewis, *A Grief Observed* (New York: Bantam Books), pages 34-35.

7. Lewis, page 35.
8. Harriet Goldhor Lerner, Ph.D., *The Dance of Anger: A Woman's Guide to Changing the Patterns of Intimate Relationships* (New York: Harper & Row, 1985).
9. Deborah Tannen, Ph.D., *You Just Don't Understand* (New York: William Morrow, 1990), page 16.
10. Tannen, page 16-17.
11. Willard F. Harley, Jr., *His Needs, Her Needs: Building an Affair-Proof Marriage* (Old Tappan, NJ: Fleming H. Revell, 1986), pages 11, 56-57.
12. Paul Tournier, *The Gift of Feeling* (Atlanta, GA: John Knox, 1979), page 100.
13. Dan Allender, "Humility: Antidote for Shame," *IBC Perspective*, vol. 2 (Morrison, CO: Institute of Biblical Counseling, 1988), page 36.

CHAPTER FOUR: WHEN GOD'S HEART BREAKS

1. In Donald P. McNeill, Douglas A. Morrison, and Henri J. M. Nouwen, *Compassion: A Reflection on the Christian Life* (Garden City, NY: Doubleday, 1982), page 18.
2. Rob Bryant, *Lord, Lift Me Up . . . and Let Me Stand* (Nashville, TN: Broadman Press, 1990), page 133.
3. *Webster's Third New International Dictionary*, s.v. "compassion."
4. *Webster's Third New International Dictionary*, s.v. "sympathy."
5. "Compassion," in *Vine's Expository Dictionary of New Testament Words* (McLean, VA: MacDonald Publishing Company, n.d.), page 220.
6. Brennan Manning, *Lion and Lamb: The Relentless Tenderness of Jesus* (Old Tappan, NJ: Fleming H. Revell, 1986), page 127.
7. In McNeill, Morrison, and Nouwen, page 16.
8. See Matthew 15:32, Mark 8:2; Matthew 9:36, Mark 6:34; Matthew 14:14, 20:34, Mark 1:41, Luke 7:13; and Luke 15:20.

9. Twila Paris, "Sing Me a Lullaby," Copyright ©1980 Singspiration Music/ASCAP. All rights reserved. Used by permission of The Benson Co., Inc., Nashville, TN.
10. Evelyn S. Bassoff, *Mothering Ourselves* (New York: Penguin Books, 1991), pages 111-119.

CHAPTER FIVE: THE PARADOX OF SOVEREIGNTY AND COMPASSION

1. Steven R. Mosley, *A Tale of Three Virtues: Cures for Colorless Christianity* (Sisters, OR: Questar Publishers, 1989), page 73.
2. Harold S. Kushner, *When Bad Things Happen to Good People* (Boston, MA: G. K. Hall, 1982), page 4.
3. Sandra D. Wilson, *Counseling Adult Children of Alcoholics* (Dallas, TX: Word, 1989), page 101.
4. See Romans 8:18 and 2 Corinthians 4:17-18.
5. See Colossians 3:3 and Luke 13:30.
6. William Blake, "On Another's Sorrow," *Eerdman's Book of Christian Poetry* (Grand Rapids, MI: Eerdmans, 1981), page 45.
7. Brennan Manning, *Lion and Lamb: The Relentless Tenderness of Jesus* (Old Tappan, NJ: Fleming H. Revell, 1986), page 160.
8. In Donald P. McNeill, Douglas A. Morrison, and Henri J. M. Nouwen, *Compassion: A Reflection on the Christian Life* (Garden City, NY: Doubleday, 1982), page 24.

CHAPTER SIX: BARRICADES OF THE NEEDY HEART

1. *Webster's Third New International Dictionary*, s.v. "self-pity."
2. David E. Carlson, *Counseling and Self-Esteem* (Waco, TX: Word, 1988), page 174.
3. Judith Viorst, *Necessary Losses* (New York: Simon and Schuster, 1986), page 251.

4. Sandra D. Wilson, *Counseling Adult Children of Alcoholics* (Dallas, TX: Word, 1989), page 73.
5. H. Norman Wright, *Always Daddy's Girl: Understanding Your Father's Impact on Who You Are* (Ventura, CA: Regal Books, 1989), page 92.
6. Wilson, page 71.
7. Wright, page 159.
8. Brennan Manning, *Lion and Lamb: The Relentless Tenderness of Jesus* (Old Tappan, NJ: Fleming H. Revell, 1986), page 130.

CHAPTER SEVEN: HOW GOD REACHES US IN OUR SILENCE

1. Sue Monk Kidd, *When the Heart Waits* (San Francisco, CA: Harper & Row, 1990), page 124.
2. From an interview with Mark Lloyd Taylor in *Steps*, Newsletter of the National Association for Christian Recovery, Winter 1990, page 7.
3. Sue Monk Kidd, "The Story-Shaped Life," *Weavings*, vol. 4, no. 1, January/February 1989, page 24.
4. Kidd, "The Story-Shaped Life," page 25.
5. Donald W. McCullough, "Why You Don't Have to Cheer Up," *Christianity Today*, 5 November 1990, page 23.
6. Ed Kerr, "You'll See a Man," Copyright © 1988 Singspiration Music/ASCAP. All rights reserved. Used by permission of The Benson Co., Inc., Nashville, TN.
7. William Styron, *Darkness Visible: A Memoir of Madness* (New York: Random House, 1990), pages 66-67.
8. Styron, page 81.
9. Oswald Chambers, *My Utmost for His Highest* (New York: Dodd, Mead, 1935), page 41.
10. Luci Shaw, *God in the Dark* (Grand Rapids, MI: Zondervan, 1989), pages 152-153.
11. Shaw, page 158.
12. Kidd, *When the Heart Waits*, page 12.

13. Kidd, page 14.
14. Frances Hodgson Burnett, *The Secret Garden* (Phila-
    delphia and New York: J. B. Lippincott Company,
    1938), page 206. The third person pronoun "one" used
    throughout the original passage has been changed to
    the second person "you" for ease in reading.

CHAPTER EIGHT: FINDING LIFE IN THE PAIN

1. Frederick Buechner, *The Magnificent Defeat* (New York:
   Harper & Row, 1985), page 127.
2. C. Austin Miles, "In the Garden," Copyright 1912,
   1940, in *Hymns for the Family of God* (Nashville, TN:
   Paragon Associates, 1976).
3. Buechner, page 127.

CHAPTER NINE: BUILDING A COMPASSIONATE
COMMUNITY

1. Sue Monk Kidd, *When the Heart Waits* (San Francisco,
   CA: Harper & Row, 1990), pages 143-144.
2. The Evangelical Free Church of Fullerton, California,
   has compiled a list of almost 500 church-based groups
   for Adult Children of Alcoholics. To receive a copy,
   send $2.00 to E.V. Free Fullerton, Attn: Dave Carder,
   2801 N. Brea Blvd., Fullerton, CA 92635.
3. There are almost five hundred New Hope groups
   nationwide. *Steps,* a quarterly newsletter published by
   The National Association for Christian Recovery (P.O.
   Box 11095, Whittier, CA 90603), provides articles and
   information relevant to Christians who are growing
   through healing the past.
4. Yokefellows, the group led by Frances Swann in our
   area, describes its purpose as "seeking to create in
   modern form the deep, satisfying fellowship of the
   early Christians, and through this fellowship to stimu-
   late greater spiritual growth." For more information,

write: Yokefellows, Incorporated, 245 El Camino Real, Millbrae, CA 94030.

The primary goal of another excellent small-group ministry, Spiritual Growth, Incorporated, is "for group members to achieve better self-understanding and self-acceptance." Secondary goals include spiritual growth, improved relationships, forgiveness, and marriage enrichment. For more information, write: Glen Reddell, Spiritual Growth, Inc., Box 64248, Lubbock, TX 79424.

5. As quoted from a telephone interview with Dr. Cecil Osborne, founder of Yokefellows, Inc., on 5 September 1991.
6. In Donald P. McNeill, Douglas A. Morrison, and Henri J. M. Nouwen, *Compassion: A Reflection on the Christian Life* (Garden City, NY: Doubleday, 1982), page 14.
7. Max Lucado, *No Wonder They Call Him Savior* (Portland, OR: Multnomah Press, 1986), page 106.

CHAPTER TEN: COMPASSION AS ENERGY

1. Brennan Manning, *Lion and Lamb: The Relentless Tenderness of Jesus* (Old Tappan, NJ: Fleming H. Revell, 1986), page 60.
2. Manning, page 128.
3. F. Kefa Sempangi, *A Distant Grief* (Glendale, CA: Regal Books, 1979), page 27.
4. Sempangi, page 51.
5. *Webster's Third New International Dictionary*, s.v. "pity."
6. Sempangi, page 134.
7. Mary Ann Bell, "They're Probably Still Singing," *Virtue*, September/October 1991, page 41.
8. Bell, page 41.

Author

Kathy Olsen is a freelance writer whose articles and poems have appeared in a number of Christian periodicals over the past five years. In 1974, she earned a Bachelor of Arts degree and did graduate work in English literature at Texas Tech University. As a student, Kathy became a Christian through a campus ministry there.

Through her leadership in women's Bible studies and participation in various support groups over the years, Kathy has had the opportunity to share her own struggle with spiritual and emotional growth. In the process, she has also "heard" the silent pain many competent Christian women experience but have difficulty talking about. Kathy lives with her husband, Lloyd, and their two sons, Brian and Mark, in Tyler, Texas.